LIBRARY OF LATIN AMERICAN
HISTORY AND CULTURE
GENERAL EDITOR:
DR. A. CURTIS WILGUS

Bust of an Inca

OLD CIVILIZATIONS

OF

INCA LAND

By CHARLES W. MEAD
LATE CURATOR OF PERUVIAN ARCHAEOLOGY

NEW YORK
COOPER SQUARE PUBLISHERS, INC.
1972

Originally Published, 1935
Reprinted 1972 by Cooper Square Publishers, Inc.
59 Fourth Avenue, New York, N. Y. 10003
International Standard Book Number 0-8154-0430-1
Library of Congress Catalog Card Number 72-85431

Printed in the United States of America

PREFACE

The author of this book died in February, 1928, after a long and honorable service as curator of South American collections. It is fitting, therefore, that we issue a new edition of this useful handbook as a guide to the collections and the literature relating to the prehistoric civilization of the Peruvian Highlands. To quote from the original preface of the author:—

"When viewing the exhibits in any museum hall the visitor is apt to derive much more information and pleasure, than he otherwise would, if he has some knowledge of the subject illustrated by the objects in the cases. This little book is written to furnish such information, rather than to be a complete guide to the Hall of Prehistoric Peru. Herein the Peruvians will tell quite a part of their own story through drawings and photographs of the works they have left behind.

"The story such objects tell is always reliable, which is more than can be said of the accounts of the earliest Spanish chroniclers, in whose narratives one is astonished to find so little information regarding the daily life of the Indians: their houses, dress, food, customs, etc. It seems that the conquerors cared nothing for these things, nor could they possibly imagine that future generations would be interested in them. Seemingly they were actuated by only two motives: the acquisition of gold and the propagation of Catholicism. When killing, or despoiling heretics of their property, they undoubtedly believed they were doing God an acceptable service, for such was the spirit of the time of the Conquest

(1532), and it is probable that the Conquistadores were above the level of the average Spaniard of that time.''

The chief recent additions to our knowledge of prehistoric Peru are certain conclusions respecting the time sequences of the several localized cultures, a chapter upon which has been supplied by Ronald L. Olson, Research Associate in Peruvian Archaeology, in the main a reprint of an article previously appearing in *Natural History*.

The Peruvian collections in the American Museum of Natural History are largely the results of excavations made by Adolph Francis Bandelier, who was in Peru and Bolivia continuously from July 1, 1892 to April 1, 1903. For the first two years Mr. Bandelier worked under the patronage of Mr. Henry Villard, after which the work was taken over by the Museum.

Among the many donors who have contributed to the accumulation of these collections are: the Guggenheim Brothers, Morris K. Jesup, A. D. Juilliard, E. P. Mathewson, J. P. Morgan, and Henry Villard.

THE EDITOR.

June 27, 1932.

CONTENTS

ILLUSTRATIONS

TEXT FIGURES

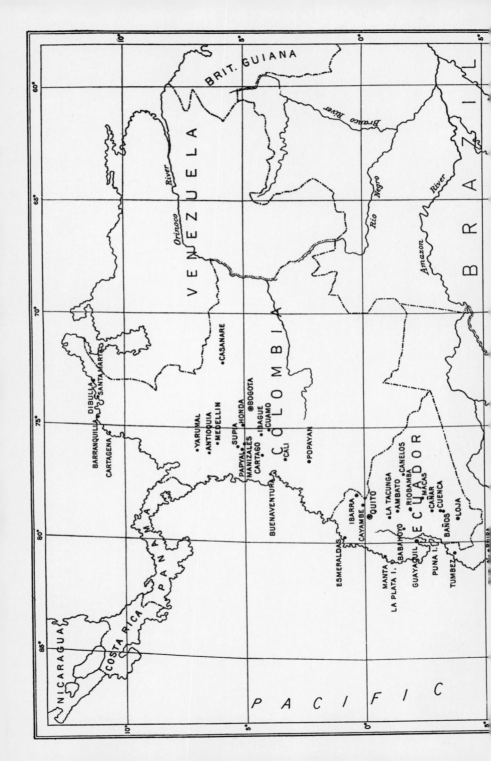

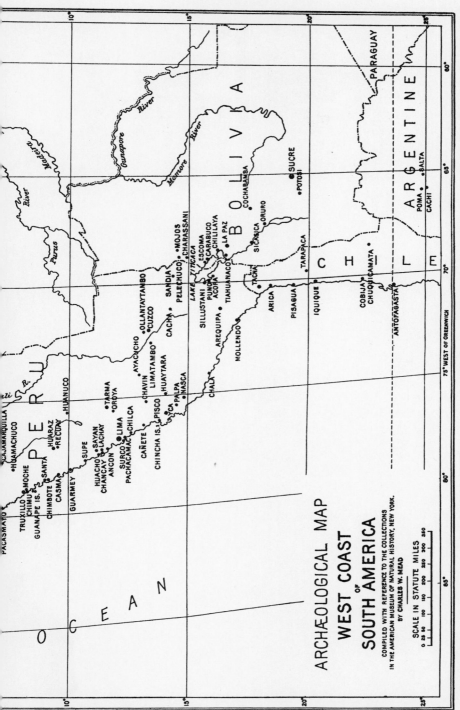

ARCHÆOLOGICAL MAP
OF
WEST COAST
OF
SOUTH AMERICA

COMPILED WITH REFERENCE TO THE COLLECTIONS
IN THE AMERICAN MUSEUM OF NATURAL HISTORY, NEW YORK.

BY CHARLES W. MEAD

SCALE IN STATUTE MILES
0 25 50 100 150 200 250 300 350

Fig. 1

Fig. 2. Map of South America, showing the Remarkable Topography of the Territory occupied by the Ancient Peruvians.

INTRODUCTION

IF one turns to a map of South America, he will notice that a strip of land averaging perhaps 40 miles in width runs along the west coast between the seashore and the base of the mountains. The parts of this narrow strip falling within the geographical limits of Peru form a desert where rain rarely falls. But high up in the mountains it does rain, sending numerous streams down their western slopes through narrow valleys in the desert belt below.

The mountains, for the most part, are in two parallel ranges: the eastern, known as the Andes; the western, or coast range, as the Cordillera. To the north and east of Lake Titicaca is the great chain of the Bolivian Andes, or Cordillera Real. All of these ranges are pierced by deep valleys through which flow most of the waters collected between the two ranges, forming uncounted streams and rivers which converge into the Amazon, the Orinoco, and the Plata.

There are said to be fifty mountain peaks over 18,000 feet above the sea in the region occupied by the old Peruvian Empire. A few of these are marked on the map (Fig. 2). Of these, the altitudes of Huascaran and Aconcagua appear to have been accurately determined; the others are variously given by different authorities.

Hugo Beck's classification of the mountains of Bolivia is the one generally accepted. He divides them as follows:—

1. The Coast Cordillera
2. The Cordillera de los Andes

9

FIG. 3. Extent of the Ancient Inca Empire.

10

3. The Cordillera Real or Bolivian Andes
4. Isolated ranges between 2 and 3
5. Ranges east of the Cordillera Real

Thus we see that, in the main, the land of the Peruvians is a succession of narrow valleys, some well watered and fertile, while others are barren wastes.

When Peru was visited by the Spaniards under Pizarro in 1532 the entire country was under the domination of the Inca of Cuzco. But the ascendancy of the Incas was preceded by a long period of development which is usually spoken of as the Megalithic Period.

Fig. 4. A Portion of the Great Fortress, Sacsahuaman, Cuzco.

Megalithic Period. All our knowledge of the Peruvians before the rise of the Inca Empire is derived from such of their works as are still extant. They were the builders of Tiahuanaco and the similar megalithic remains found in many parts of the country. Among the best known of these megalithic structures are Sacsahuaman, on the hill above Cuzco, Ollantaytambo, at Concacha near Apurimac, Huiñaque, Chavin, Huaraz and Quecap (Kuelap) in Chachapoyas. Remains of this type are widely distributed over the whole country, suggesting that their builders were a more or less homogeneous people. Prescott (Vol. 1, 33) well says of them:—

Who this race were and whence they came may afford a tempting theme for inquiry to the speculative antiquarian. But it is a land of darkness that lies far beyond the domain of history.

Yet due to painstaking archaeological research we know there were three great centers of culture in Peru in prehistoric times: the regions about Trujillo, Nazca, and Tiahuanaco. There is every reason

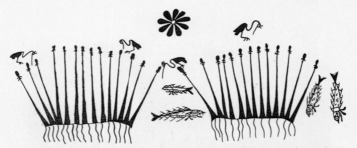

Fig. 5. Painting on a Pottery Vessel depicting Rushes and Their Roots, Fish swimming among the Rushes, and Birds flying above them.

to believe that these cultures flourished, at least in a portion of their duration, at the same time, for we find forms in pottery and ornamental motives in each that also appear in the other two. Notwithstanding this, the characteristics of their arts were entirely different. In the northern coast, or Trujillo art, realism prevailed to a greater extent than in any other part of the Empire: animal and vegetable forms in terra cotta, without conventionalization, vases that were evidently intended as portraits, and even well executed landscapes and scenes from their daily life occur. These paintings are generally in reddish brown on the cream-colored slip which was commonly applied to their pottery. Sometimes a number of colors were used.

The art of the Nazca region does not show the wonderful modeling found at Trujillo; in fact, in this respect, it is inferior to that of many parts of

Fig. 6. A Portrait Vase in Terra Cotta, from a Grave in Chepen, Peru. Trujillo Culture.

Peru, but in the wealth of color it surpasses all other regions. Conventionalization runs riot in the painted decorations of the pottery.

The art of Tiahuanaco is best illustrated in work in stone. Perhaps the best and most characteristic example is the carving on the great monolithic gateway at Akapana. The central figure will be found in Fig. 8. It has been much injured by time and

FIG. 7. A Brilliantly Colored Pottery Vessel from Nazca, Peru. The design shows conventionalized humming birds gathering honey from six-pointed flowers.

vandals, especially about the head. A few words about the decorative designs on the representation of this god will be in place, as these and variants of them are known in nearly all parts of the country. The design motives are the human figure, the con-

FIG. 8. The Central Figure on the Great Stone Gateway at Akapana, Tiahuanaco. The two puma heads at the top have been added
for comparison; the one at the left is from a textile; at the right is
one modeled in clay as a handle for a pottery vessel.

dor, and the puma, each highly conventionalized. The central ray of the headdress, above the god's head, terminates in a human head. Those at the extreme right and left, both top and bottom, and the central ray on either side represent a puma head. Human, puma, and condor heads decorate the poncho and the belt which confines it terminates at both ends with a puma head.

In either hand the god holds some sort of ceremonial staff. The lower end is carved to represent the head of the male condor while the upper end is bifurcated and has two female condor heads. Whether or not Tiahuanaco art, as many believe, is the oldest in western South America, its influence extended over the greater part of the region later occupied by the Inca Empire. This is particularly the case in some coast localities. The decorations on textiles and pottery from Ancon and Pachacamac abound in these queer puma and condor heads of Tiahuanaco.

Inca Period. While nothing is definitely known about the rise of the Inca Empire it seems probable that it had its origin in the joining of two Andine Megalithic cultures, that of Tiahuanaco and the Urubamba Valley. This conclusion seems to be borne out by both the forms and ornamental designs on pottery from ancient burial places in the Coast valleys which are often in the styles of Cuzco and Tiahuanaco.

The Incas domesticated the llama which they used as a beast of burden. This gave them a great advantage over their enemies, as it enabled them to transport supplies to a great distance. By conquest and confederation they gradually overran the entire country. It was probably about 1400 A.D. that they finally conquered the northern coast region. So, finally, the Empire of the Incas included what is now Ecuador, Peru, Bolivia, and Northern Chile, and extended from the second degree of north latitude to the Maule River, in Chile, a distance of 2300 miles along the coast.

The government, however mild in character, was a pure despotism. The Inca, or chief ruler, as the representative of the Sun, was at the head of the

FIG. 9. Typical Inca or Cuzco Forms in Pottery.

priesthood and of the army, making all the laws, and appointing judges to enforce them. In short, he was a superior being, owning everything, and the source of all power in the Empire. No one could approach him unless barefoot and carrying some token of homage.

The amount of credit that can be placed in Indian traditions or statements of the earliest Peruvian historians, gathered from such traditions, is made

clear if we attempt to give a list of the reigning
Incas.   The list of Blas Valera contains one hundred names.   Now if we assume that each reign
lasted twenty-five or twenty-seven years it takes us
back to 950 B.C.   Others give much smaller numbers, and one, only eight names.   A number of
authors who have written during the last decade
believe that the first Inca began his reign during the
twelfth century.

From the foregoing it is evident that the time is
not yet ripe to fix dates with any degree of certainty,
and that we must wait until much more intensive
field-work and study of the available literature has
been accomplished.   Even then, from the nature of
the problem, its solution is doubtful.

Bandelier (p. 288) says:—

Inca chronology is far from trustworthy previous to the time of
the chief Tupac Yupanqui, but from that time on a reasonable
approximation to the dates becomes possible.

Tupac Yupanqui was succeeded by Huayna Capac
who died in 1525, only seven years before Pizarro
began his conquest.

Sir Martin Conway made his successful attempt
to climb Mount Illimani in 1898.   On his way down
he met Mr. Bandelier, whom he describes as the
Flinders Petrie of prehistoric Peru and Bolivia.
Mr. Bandelier was engaged, at the time, in excavat-
ing ruined houses on the flanks of Illimani, for the
American Museum.   Sir Martin asked him:—

"Were the ancient dwellers on Illimani Incas?:"   I ignorantly
asked. . . . "I don't know.   I have no theories.   I know nothing
about Incas.   All I know is that throughout Peru and Bolivia there
were ancient inhabitants, for whom I have no name—prehistoric
Peruvian, if you like.   These people left remains which exist, and

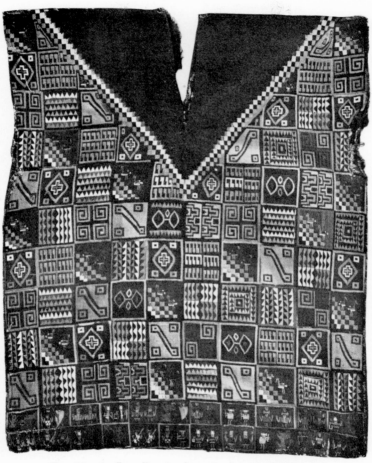

FIG. 10. An Inca Poncho from the Island of Titicaca

descendants—the Indians we see about us. The remains show that
there were great varieties of local habit and custom—whether the
result of racial variety or merely of different conditions of life, I
don't know. What we do is to investigate the remains and discover
facts; we record the facts and leave inferences and generalizations to
other people. There are not facts enough discovered yet to warrant
very general inferences. Some day there may be, but it will need
much more excavation first. Our investigation is twofold. We dig
into the ground, and we dig into the minds of the living people. The
Indian to-day is very little altered by European influence. He carries a thin varnish of Christianity, but below it are the pre-Columbian
beliefs and superstitions practically entire. . . . ''   (Pp. 147–148.)

Historians agree that the Inca was of a different
physical type from the common people of his time,
or the Peruvian Indians of today: a result of generations of culture and rule.   The color of his skin
was many shades lighter than the present Peruvian
Indians, nose only slightly aquiline, chin and mouth
firm, and the whole face majestic and refined.   The
ceremonial headdress of the Inca was a golden semi-
circular mitre, under the front of which was the red
fringe on his forehead.   Over the golden mitre rose
two white and black feathers and in the lobes of his
ears were very large golden earplugs.   Over his
poncho the Inca wore a sort of mantle, both garments made of vicuña wool.   A broad belt confined
the poncho at the waist.   His breast ornament of
gold represented the sun.   The breeches terminated
in loose folds at the knees.   On his feet he wore a
kind of sandal.

The Inca, equipped for war, carried a shield and
either a warclub or battle ax of copper or bronze.
The royal prince was well trained for the position
of Inca.   At about sixteen years of age, he, with
other princes of the blood, was obliged to undergo

a severe training and military probation to prove his strength, courage, and general fitness to govern the empire. The masters and judges were men famous in war and well versed in all matters of government.

To test their strength and endurance they were made to fast for six days, with only a few handfuls of unbaked corn with a small jar of water, as such a fast might be necessary in times of war. Among other tests they were obliged to run a race over a distance of a league and a half. Garcilasso (Chap. XXIV–XXV) says their parents and relations would intercept the runners, encouraging them, and telling them it was better to break their hearts in the race than to come off with dishonor.

One day the novices would be divided into two equal parts: one to garrison the fortress, and the other to assault it. The following day they changed stations. Their strength, agility, and understanding of the art of war was judged by the outcome of these trials. Their reputations being at stake they fought with such heat that, although they used blunted weapons, many were wounded, and often some were killed. Those who successfully passed these trials were obliged to show their dexterity in archery, throwing stones at a mark with the sling, casting the lance and dart, and in short, in the use of every war weapon. They were also obliged to learn how to make, with their own hands, all implements of war, and their clothing.

Beginning of the Historical Period. If we divide the range of the world's culture into enlightened, civilized, barbarous, savage, and pre-savage. as suggested by many writers, the Peruvians, at the

time of the Conquest, come under the head of barbarous peoples, if one defines barbarism as a stage
in which powerful nations were founded and sys-
tems of record developed.

It is not uncommon for a barbarous people to
reach a high development in one of the arts, as for
instance, in basketry, but the Peruvians excelled in
many directions.   They produced great architects,
as shown in many of their structures, and great
engineers, who built aqueducts hundreds of miles
long for irrigating the desert coast lands.   They
made pottery in beautiful forms, colors, and decoration, and textiles which, in technique and design,
have never been excelled, if indeed, they have ever
been equaled.   They invented the *quipu,* an efficient
instrument for keeping their accounts.   They had a
well organized government.

These things seem to entitle them to be classed as
a civilized nation; but the other side of the picture
is not so agreeable.   We are told in one paragraph
that the Inca was a most beneficent ruler, and in the
next, that he was a savage, who being offended at an
individual, immediately proceeded to destroy the
village to which the offender belonged, killing men,
women, and children.

Reading Prescott's "Conquest of Peru" leaves
one with the impression that the Incas, at the
time of the Spanish invasion, were making remarkable strides toward becoming a highly enlightened
nation.   We now suspect that when Pizarro entered
the country they had reached the highest development it was possible for them to attain, and were, in
fact, at the beginning of a period of retrogression.

Historical contact of the Peruvians with almost every Eastern people has been claimed to account for many of their arts; but none of these claims has been substantiated. So it is now generally conceded that they developed in their own country and owe little to any outside influence. Every artifact so far taken from old graves in Peru bears the distinctive native mark. For instance, place a Peruvian pottery vessel with a hundred vessels from as many other localities, and one familiar with native Peruvian work could pick it out at a glance.

Again Mexico and Peru flourished at the same time, but it is improbable that they knew of each other's existence. Certainly their arts developed along very different lines. The character of their cultural achievements was entirely different, for while the Peruvians were much superior in agriculture, the textile arts, and in the construction of such public works as roads, canals, and aqueducts, they fell far short of the Maya in the higher intellectual culture; more particularly in astronomy, and in the invention of hieroglyphs as a means of communicating thoughts by visible symbols.

As stated before, the rule of the Incas extended over the present borders of Ecuador on the north to Chile on the south. Unfortunately, we have no satisfactory knowledge as to what peoples inhabited Chile and Ecuador before the Incas began to rule, for though a number of the old Spanish chroniclers have made statements on this subject, their sources of information were native traditions. Naturally their accounts do not agree and are otherwise unreliable. However, our archaeological knowledge of Ecuador and Chile indicates that the pre-Inca Megalithic people of Peru did not extend so far. It is true that occasionally in old graves both to the north and the south of Peru one finds a piece of Megalithic Peruvian pottery that had been carried along by trade, but the usual finds in Ecuador are quite different from those in Peru and also in Chile. The indications are, therefore, that from the beginning, Ecuador, Peru, and Chile, were three fairly distinct culture provinces.

Physical Type. It is obvious that the physical type of the prehistoric Peruvians can be determined only from the skeletal remains in their graves. Although there is an abundance of such material in museums not much somatological work has been done; even the present Indians have received but little attention. After a visit to Peru, where he collected several thousand skulls and skeletons, Dr. Aleš Hrdlička says:—

It can now be positively stated that the whole coast of Peru, at least from Pisco well south of Pachacamac, to Pacasmayo north of the valley of Chicama, was peopled by one and the same type of natives, the brachycephalic (short-headed) Indian of moderate stature. (Smithsonian Miscellaneous Collections, vol. 56, No. 16, p. 10).

In the same paper Dr. Hrdlička states that the present Indians as far south as the southern confines of Peru are also of this type; but farther south at Arica and along the Chilean coast there is found an increasingly large proportion of dolichocephalic natives. From the northern extremity of the central part of the Chilean territory and southward this latter type is the only one encountered.

In the Aymara region of Bolivia the skulls in the most ancient graves show but one form of artificial deformation, the "flathead" type. Although occipital flattening seems to have been the general form in the north, quite a number of the "flathead" type have been found in the very early graves.   Such deformation of the skull was probably brought about by means of boards and ligatures placed on the infant's head shortly after birth, and not removed for a very considerable length of time.

The present Indians of Peru and Bolivia may be described as of moderate stature, the men measuring between 5 feet 2 inches and 5 feet 3 inches, the women about 2 inches less.

CHAPTER I
HOUSEHOLD ARTS AND INDUSTRIES

Food, Fishing, and Hunting. The flesh of the deer, llama, and the guinea pig, and in some localities, the tapir, peccary, and the *vischacha,* a large rodent, ducks, geese, and the *yutu,* a kind of partridge, constituted the principal animal food. The coast peoples subsisted quite largely on fish. The sea all along the coast abounded in a great variety of excellent fish. The inland lakes and rivers also furnished an abundant supply.

FIG. 11. A Water Vessel in the Form of a Guinea Pig. In many localities the flesh of the guinea pig is the only meat. It is roasted or made into a thin stew, highly seasoned with Chili peppers.

Fish were captured in nets by hook and line, and with spears having barbed stone or copper points. Many of these spears were made with stout shafts and detachable points to which were fastened long cords or strips of llama skin, by which the points, after they left the shaft, could be recovered.

Hunting implements were the same as those used in war: the bow and arrow, the club with stone or copper head, a heavy spear, sometimes cast with a throwing stick, and the bolas.

In many parts of the country, the only large animal that the common people could hunt was the deer. The herds of wild vicuña and alpaca on the mountains belonged to the Inca who caused the people to

26

assemble once every four years and drive these animals into an enclosure, where they were captured by
thousands.   They were sheared for their wool; a
certain number were killed and their skins and flesh
divided among the people; the rest were allowed to
escape.

Agriculture.   Agriculture may be said to have
been carried on in a strictly scientific way, often
under great natural difficulties. Arable land, in many
parts, was not for every one.
To remedy this shortage the
hillsides were terraced and
soil laboriously carried up.

To prepare the soil for
planting a stout stick was
used, sometimes provided
with a cross piece by which
the foot could force it into the
ground.   The plow was unknown in aboriginal America,
but early historians tell us
that in Peru a pointed stick
was sometimes drawn through
the earth by a number of men
with a rope, the women following to break up the clods.
Stone clod-breakers and stone
hoes will be found in the Museum collection. On the northern coast, the digging-stick

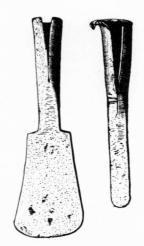

Fig. 12. Agricultural Im-
plements of Copper. Wood-
en handles were driven into
the sockets.

was shod with copper.   This copper point, shaped
much like a chisel, had a socket at the upper end into
which the handle was driven (See Fig. 12).

The prehistoric Peruvians were well versed in the use of manures, using for this purpose guano, from the islands off the coast, and small fish, particularly a sardine, which they could procure in immense numbers.

They had a remarkable system of irrigation which brought into existence fertile fields in the desert coast region where otherwise no vegetation could exist. Water from mountain streams and lakes was brought by canals from a great distance and carried down into the lowlands where it was distributed in all required directions in small streams. The ruins of these irrigation works still exist. An old reservoir in the Valley of Nepena is three-fourths of a mile long by more than half a mile broad and has a massive stone dam eighty feet thick. At Chimbote, a short distance inland from the Bay of Ferrol, was an aqueduct from the Santa River, sixteen miles distant. The greater part of this fine work still exists, and is computed to have a capacity of sixty million cubic feet of water daily.

Besides maize, potatoes, sweet potatoes, tomatoes, beans, manioc, squashes, oca, quinoa, and two varieties of cotton, we know that other vegetables and quite a variety of fruits were cultivated, because they are either found in graves, or exact representations in pottery are extant. No one has compiled a complete list of these products, nor has it been possible to identify all the fruits and vegetables reproduced in ornamental pottery forms, but a reasonably complete list is given in the table on page 29.

Yet, clearly to understand the agricultural resources of Peru one must take note of the fact that the high narrow mountain chains, with their narrow

List of Important Plants Cultivated in Peru before the Discovery of America by Columbus in 1492

Agave	*Agave americana*, Linn.
Alligator pear	*Persea gratissima*, R. P.
Bean, kidney	*Phaseolus vulgaris*, Linn.
Bean, lima	*Phaseolus lunatus*, Linn., var. *macro carpus*, Benth.
Coca (cocaine)	*Erythroxylum coca*, Lamarck
Cherimoya	*Anona cherimolia*, Miller
Chili Pepper	*Capsicum annuum*, Linn.
Cotton	*Gossypium barbadense*, Linn.
Guava	*Psidium guayava*, Raddi
Maize or Indian corn	*Zea mays*, Linn.
Manioc, bitter	*Manihot utilissima*, Pohl.
Manioc, sweet	*Manihot aipi*, Pax.
Peanut	*Arachis hypogea*, Linn.
Potato	*Solanum tuberosum*, Linn.
Oca	*Oxalis tuberosa*, Molina
Quinine	*Chinchona officinalis*, Linn.
Quinoa	*Chenopodium quinoa*, Wild.
Sweet potato	*Ipomosa batatas*, Poir.
Squash	*Cucurbita maxima*, Duchesne
Tobacco	*Nicotiana tabacum*, Linn.
Tomato	*Lycopersicum esculentum*, Mill.

deep valleys, bring close together different ranges
of temperature and moisture, and that, in consequence, the agricultural products of Peru as a whole
will be rich in variety and form. Quinoa, for example, can be raised upon very high ground, where
the bleak winds and low temperatures make the
growing of maize impossible. Further, one may
reasonably expect that the homely agricultural arts
of the present are not materially different from
what they were in prehistoric days. Thus, about
Lake Titicaca is grown a variety of small potato
which the natives freeze and then press, to free it
from water. Thus prepared, it is called *chuñu*.
It is a tasteless food, but the only way the potato
can be preserved in that climate. Again, the present-
day Indians, when starting on a journey, generally
take with them no other food than corn, roasted and
ground. A spoonful of this meal and a swallow of
water, now and then, is all they require. That both
these foods were popular in prehistoric times is
indicated by their presence in graves, especially the
latter, which· is often found with the dead, as if to
sustain the departed upon a long journey.

Household Utensils. The ancient Peruvians as
indicated by the remains in old burial places, did not
possess a great variety of household implements and
utensils. We find the stone metate with its hand
stone, used in grinding corn; also stone mortars and
pestles. The ancient Peruvians had gourd vessels,
many of them beautifully decorated in pyrography,
but pottery vessels were in more common use.

All the cooking, except such as could be done on
the coals of a fire, seems to have been done in these
vessels. In the Museum's collection are many cook-

ing pots with soot still adhering to their bottoms.
One notes also a large number of saucer-shaped vessels and spoons of terra cotta, wood, silver and copper.   They had no substitute for knives and forks
unless we except the *topu,* or shawl pin of copper or
bronze, the large thin head of which is often used by
the present Indians as a knife.

Large pottery vessels were used for holding water
or for storing corn.   The largest storage jar in the
Museum collections is four feet high and nearly as
much in diameter.   From this size these vessels
range downward to a tiny pot half an inch high.
This great range in size, as one may suspect, accom-
panies a multiplicity of pottery forms.

Drinking cups, bowls, and saucer-like vessels of
gold and silver are frequently observed in collections.   These were undoubtedly used by the Inca or
his nobility, in religious ceremonies, or buried with
the dead for use in a future life.

Pottery. As just noted, the Peruvians reached a
high degree of skill in the potter's art.   The potter's wheel was unknown in pre-Columbian America.
Vessels were largely made by the coiling process: a
long strip of prepared clay was coiled round for the
foundation, and as successive coils were added, the
material was pressed down to make the mass adhere,
and the fingers, a shell, smooth pebble, or other small
implement, employed to mould the vessel into the
desired shape, and to obliterate all outward signs of
the coiling.   The vessel was then dried in the sun,
polished with a smooth pebble, painted, and fired.
In some regions pottery vessels were cast in two
moulds, one for the upper half and another for the
lower.   After the two parts had been joined the

Fig. 13. Reproductions of Squashes in Clay. Trujillo Culture.

32

place of contact was so nicely smoothed over that it
cannot ordinarily be observed on the outside, but is
plainly visible in broken vessels.   Peruvian pottery
has always been admired for the beauty of its lines,
and for the forms and colors of its decorative designs.   Further, we owe to the old potters of Peru
much of the information we have concerning things
familiar to them in their daily life, as the illustrations in this book show.   Thus, for example, the vessels shown in Fig. 13 are clear evidence that the
squash was cultivated.   Many other examples of
vegetable and animal forms could be given if space
permitted.

Baskets.   In the graves of women are generally
found their work baskets.   These were used to hold
weaving, netting, and sewing implements; needles of
thorn or copper, cones of cotton, spindles, balls of
thread, and also various nicknacks.   Other forms of
baskets have been found, but apparently the Peruvians did not use baskets for many purposes.

Most of the work baskets are shaped like the one
shown in Fig. 14, but occasionally a rectangular one
is found.   The original of the illustration was made
by plaiting rushes over thin slats of split cane.
These slats are so placed that they form horizontal
bands around the basket, and cross it lengthwise on
top and bottom.   Over the slats five parallel rush
strands pass diagonally, and reverse their diagonal
direction.   Between the bands we have a regular
two-leaf twill plaiting.   At the edge one set of diagonal rush strand turns out, and at right angles runs
back into the body plaiting, while the second set
turns in at right angles and enters the body plaiting.

Some objects found in these baskets give us some insight into the character and tastes of their owners. For example, they often contain a child's doll in process of making. This would seem to confirm the statements of early writers that the Peruvians were very fond of their children. Again, the basket shown in the illustrations contains a handful of peanuts, which brings to our mind the picture of a woman sitting at her loom eating these nuts.

Fig. 14. A Woman's Work Basket, containing Yarns, Spindles, Needles, etc., exactly as buried with the Owner.

Plaited mats are very common, ranging from very coarse to very fine weaving. They were used as sleeping mats, as partitions in the houses, as outside wrappings for mummy bundles, and, in the desert coast region, to cover the sticks placed across the tops of graves to protect the body from falling sand. The weaving technique of these mats is twilled plaiting.

Dress. Among the old historians Father Bernabé Cobo and Cieza de Leon have left us the most complete descriptions of the clothing worn by Peruvian Indians at the time of the Conquest. From their accounts it appears that the dress of a man consisted of a breech-cloth, over which was worn a poncho, a sort of shirt, with or without sleeves, called *uncu*. The outer garment, shaped like a blanket, was thrown over the shoulders. This was called *yacolla*. When dancing or at work two of the corners were tied together at the left shoulder. The men carried cloth bags hung by a strap about the neck. These took the place of pockets and were usually filled with coca leaves.

In some localities the women wrapped themselves in a large piece of cloth which hung under the arms. The edges were pulled up over the shoulders and fastened with a pin (*topu*). A broad belt (*chumpi*) encircled the waist. The outer mantle was thrown over the shoulders and fastened over the breast with a pin. This shawl-like garment was called *lliclla*.

The bronze pins that fastened their clothing had very large heads; some were in the form of spoons with which they ate their roasted and ground corn; others had flat heads, sharpened on the edge, and were used as knives.

On going to sleep at night they never undressed; the men merely threw off the *yacolla* and the women the *lliclla*. When any foot covering was used it was a sandal made of llama hide or of braided vegetable fiber. (See Fig. 15.)

FIG. 15. A Water Vessel in the Form of a Human Foot, showing the Type of Sandal worn, and the Method of fastening to the Foot.

FIG. 16. Peruvian Costume depicted on a Pottery Vessel. The man wears a poncho with sleeves and a shawl-like garment (yacolla) over it.

Personal Ornaments. The Spaniards called the Inca and his relatives *orejones* (big ears) from their custom of piercing their ears and enlarging the hole until the lobe hung down nearly to the shoulders. The material of which the ear ornament was made and its size varied according to the rank of the wearer and was regulated by law. These ear ornaments are common objects in collections from the old graves. They are of all sizes and variously made of gold, silver, clay, wood, and canes. (For ear ornaments in use, see the Frontispiece.)

They used an endless variety of beads made of various kinds of stone, bone, shell, seeds, and berries. Gold and silver beads were common; we also find them made of precious and semiprecious stones, emerald, lapis lazuli, amethyst, turquoise, smithsonite, agate, and quartz.

Broad bands of very thin gold, often with embossed decoration, were sometimes worn as wrist ornaments, and circular or square pieces of silver pierced near the edges with holes, were sewed to garments and belts. Finger rings were not uncommon. A mummy hand and forearm, with a ring on the second finger and a bracelet on the arm will be found in the Museum collection.

Combs were worn as hair ornaments and many will be found on exhibition. The teeth in these combs, which are either of thorns or cane, are held in position by interwoven yarns, forming a tightly woven fabric, ornamented usually with bird or fish figures.

In collections of gold and silver objects are many human figurines. Some of these represent women with their hair in one braid and others in two. Ulloa

(Vol. 2, p. 13) in describing the Indian women of
Sechura, says:—

> The condition of everyone may be known by their manner of dress-
> ing their hair, maids and widows dividing it into two plaited locks,
> one hanging on each shoulder, whilst married women braid all their
> hair in one.

These prehistoric figurines indicate that these distinctive methods of dressing the hair survived from
pre-Spanish times.

Textiles. Thousands of pre-Inca graves in the
dry, nitrous sand of the Peruvian coast have perfectly preserved for us textiles woven more than a
thousand years ago. Many of these webs are as
strong and their colors as bright as they were when
taken from the primitive looms. These textiles ap-
peal to the artist not only because of the great
beauty of their color schemes but for their strange
conventionalized animal figures. Designers and design students, have long sought inspiration from
them for decorative designs for silks, carpets, wall
papers, book covers, etc. Furthermore, textile man-
ufacturers and experts are astonished at the perfect
spinning of the yarns, the great variety of tech-
niques, and the unusual skill of the weavers.

William S. Murphy in his standard work, *Textile
Industries,* says of Peruvian threads:—

> It may be that the makers of Cashmere shawls, Dacca muslins,
> Aztec veils, and Peruvian robes inherited the long labors of a thou-
> sand generations; but so far as the spinners of what we call modern
> civilization are concerned the ideal has been realized, and belongs
> rather to the past than to the present or to the immediate future.
> The perfect thread is not to seek; it has been made.   (Vol. 3, 83.)

Considering that the Peruvians reached this high
standard without direct contact with any outside

people we may well endorse the statement that "It is the most extraordinary textile development of a prehistoric people."

The Peruvians had two kinds of native cotton; one pure white, the other a golden brown.   The white

FIG. 17.   A Pre-Inca Tapestry Poncho.   Pachacamac.   The warps are cotton, the wefts, vicuña wool.   The three human figures in the center are surrounded by cat, bird, and fish designs.

fiber is very even in diameter, has a greater number of convolutions per inch than the brown, and averages from 1 to 1¾ inches in length; the brown ½ inch less.   Carding was probably accomplished with the fingers; the spinning with a spindle weighted by a whorl.

In addition to cotton, wool was used.   For the most part, the wool came from three members of the camel family: the alpaca, the vicuña, and the llama.

Most of us are familiar with alpaca wool. That of the vicuña is much finer, very silky in appearance, but that of the llama is coarse, and only used in garments of the poorer class of people. Finally, the old Peruvian weavers used a bast fiber made from the maguey plant.

FIG. 18. Methods of Weaving from a Painting on a Pottery Vessel, Trujillo (After Tello). A tapestry is being woven. On the ground beside the weavers may be seen, the weaving patterns, spindles with yarns of various colors, and water jars.

The Peruvian loom consisted of two sticks, one at the top, the other at the bottom, over which the warps were stretched. In the common type of loom a heald rod lifted every other thread, forming the shed or opening for the passage of the spindle carrying the weft or filling thread. The only other implement used was the weave sword for beating up the weft threads. When tapestry was to be made the warps were stretched in the same way. No heald rod was used, a weave dagger opening the small sheds and pressing down the wefts. As many bobbins had to be used as there were to be colors in the finished web. Mr. M. D. C. Crawford, the well known textile expert, is our authority for many of the statements made here. After a long and careful study of the Peruvian textiles in the Museum's collection he says:—

In tapestry Peru reached its highest textile development. The harmony of color, the beauty and fastness of the dyes, and the perfection of the spinning and weaving, place these fabrics in a class by themselves, not only as compared to other textiles of this land, but as regards those of any other people.

A painting on a pottery vessel (Fig. 18) from the Valley of Chicama (Trujillo culture) shows women weaving. The cords of the upper loom bar are fastened to one of the house posts, the lower to the belt around the weaver's waist. The technique employed here has been called bobbin weave, which differs from ordinary tapestry in that the weft goes over and under unequal instead of equal groups of warp. In this weave the only implement required is the bobbin and there must be as many bobbins as there are colors in the finished web. Thus on the ground beside the weaver (the painter knew nothing of perspective) are the bobbins required for the work in hand, a board or other object bearing the pattern

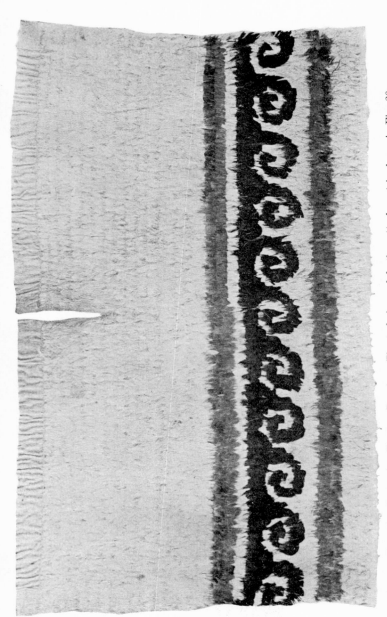

FIG. 19. Part of a Feather Poncho. The technique of feather attachment is shown in Fig. 20.

42

she is weaving, and also cups and jars for water or *chicha,* a kind of beer, which was the common drink of the country.

Feather-Work. Many of the headdresses and ponchos of feather-work found on mummies and in graves are works of art. The feather poncho is a shirt of cotton cloth, decorated with designs made by attaching differently .colored feathers to it. These feathers are strung on strings that are as long as the poncho is wide. A string so prepared is placed horizontally across the garment and sewed to it. The second string of feathers is added to overlap in shingle fashion, and so on. The design had to be carefully planned out from the beginning, and the variously colored feathers so strung on the strings as to form the design very crudely.

In the feather poncho shown in Fig. 19 the groundwork is yellow. The chief decoration is the row of scrolls in black; the others are narrow lines of red and blue. When the garment was completely covered

Fig. 20. Feather-work Technique. Method of attaching feathers to the poncho in Fig. 19.

with feathers many of the black scrolls were covered in places by the yellow feathers. These overlapping ends were trimmed away, with some cutting instrument, leaving the lines sharp and clear. Again, beautiful mosaic work was. produced by gluing small bits of feathers to cloth and wool.

Metallurgy. The knowledge of metallurgy is often taken as an index of the degree of civilization attained by a people. However this may be, a glance at a good museum collection from Peru reveals work

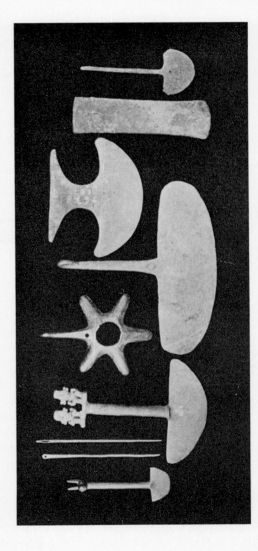

Fig. 21. Implements of Copper and Bronze. From left to right: a bronze knife; two copper needles; a bronze knife, a bronze club head and battle ax combined; two copper knives; a bronze chisel; and a copper topu, or shawl pin.

44

in gold, silver, copper, and lead. Further, the objects fashioned of these metals show that casting in moulds, beating up tall cups from a single piece, soldering, and even plating or gilding one metal with another were understood. All this indicates a high

FIG. 22. Silverwork: Hollow Figures in Thin Silver. The upper figure represents an alpaca; the lower, a llama. Island of Titicaca.

level of achievement in the metal arts. Gold was mined, but it is probable that the greater part was

washed from the gravels of rivers that flowed from
the Cordillera. In the dry season, when the water
was low, stone dams were laid across a section of the
stream, thus retaining much of the gold brought
down when the rains and melting snow turned it into
a raging torrent. The washing was done during the
next dry season.

Silver was mined in great quantity. The chief
supply seems to have come from the Potosi region.
Hundreds of partly filled excavations in various sections of the country, particularly in Bolivia, attest
to the extent of these mining operations. These excavations are merely pits in the earth, as the prehistoric Peruvians had no means of sinking deep shafts.

In addition to the metals noted above some use
was made of quicksilver and vermilion. However,
it does not appear that they employed quicksilver to
form amalgams in their mining operations until
after the coming of the Spaniards but they did use
vermilion as a red paint. Acosta (238) says:—

I speak for the Inguas Kings of Peru, and for the natural Indians,
which have laboured and digged long in these mines of quicksilver,
not knowing what quicksilver was, seeking only for Cinabrium, or
vermilion, which they call Limpi, the which they esteem much for
that effect that Plinie reports of the Romans and Ethiopians, that
is, to paint the face and bodies of themselves and their idols.

Copper is found in almost every part of the country. Bolivia is very rich in tin, ranking second only
to the Malay Peninsula in its output of this metal,
though Bolivian tin is mostly in the form of cas-
siterite. Some use was made of lead, especially in
making bolas, but no iron, before the coming of
Europeans.

The Peruvians had discovered, in prehistoric times, the art of making bronze. They found that a combination of copper and tin made a much harder and more serviceable tool than one of copper alone. A great number of these bronze implements are exhibited in the Museum collections and over two hundred of them have small labels attached which give the exact amount of copper and tin in the specimen.

FIG. 23. The Method of Working Gold and Silver. (After Benzoni, 1541–1556.)

For smelting metals cylindrical pottery furnaces called *guayras* were used. The furnace tenders had no bellows, but used copper pipes through which to blow the fire. When the ores were refractory, a number of these pipes were used at the same time.

In the Potosi region, where there was most of the time a high wind, the *guayra* was placed on some elevated spot to take advantage of this natural blast. If one is disposed to doubt the efficacy of such smelting equipment he should note the statement of W. Gowland, Professor of Metallurgy at the Royal School of Mines, England:—

Then as regards the metallic ores which were within the reach of prehistoric man, they were undoubtedly those which occur at the surface of the ground, i.e., when a mineral vein outcrops or is exposed. Now the ores which occur in this part of a vein are as a rule oxides and carbonates, which are of all ores the most easily reducible to metal, and from all these metals can be obtained without any difficulty whatever by treating them in the primitive 'hole in the ground' furnace. (*Journal of the Anthropological Institute of Great Britain and Ireland*, vol. XLIX, p. 76.)

This seems the proper place to call attention to a widespread error since many people seek tempered copper tools in the Museum collections. They may even have read of the lost art of tempering copper in Peru. The truth is that there never was such an art. The Peruvians often smelted tin with copper, forming bronze. Since this compound is much harder than copper it undoubtedly gave rise to this old belief. Yet when one subjects these old tools to chemical analysis, they prove to be alloys. So one can safely say that the Peruvians were at least on the threshold of a bronze age when conquered by Spain.

Chapter II

BUILDING AND ARCHITECTURE

Houses and Shelters. Peruvian houses were of various kinds. On the coast and in the warm valleys they were mostly low huts of cane, generally supported by posts of algarroba wood, and often plastered with a coating of mud. The roof was a mat of reeds or thatch of *ichu* grass laid over sticks. Sometimes the huts were built of adobe instead of cane, but these were roofed in the same way. In the cold

Fig. 24   Fig. 25

Fig. 24.   Model of a House on a Pottery Vessel.
Fig. 25.   The Type of Shelter used by Herders—A Clay Model.

districts stone was generally used as building material. Commonly these huts had but a single room, but occasionally they were divided into several compartments by walls of cane or adobe. Fig. 24 shows a model of a house on a pottery vessel. When possible the old Peruvians liked to build their houses on terraces. The step form figures on the side of the jar in the illustration denote such terraces.

Simple shelters were erected in the fields by shepherds to protect themselves from the elements while watching their flocks. Similar shelters are still used by the present Indian shepherds, and are a familiar sight in Bolivia (Fig. 25).

Stone Work. While the Peruvians were skilled in stone work and did, on occasion, construct massive walls, they have left behind no such elaborate structures, or such ornate sculptures as did the natives of Mexico and Central America. Their chief distinction lay in the ability to dress and handle immense blocks of stone. Yet, none but stone tools have ever been found, if we except bronze, with which the immense blocks of such hard stone as granite and andesite could have been worked into form. Some of the bronze tools in the collection, like small crowbars in shape, are bent, and the points are very dull and turned up, while the upper ends are spread out by blows of stone hammers. These may have been used in working stone. There is, however, little doubt that the chief reliance for the greater part of the work was on stone tools, as the bronze implements were not hard enough, and would have to be resharpened after a few hammer blows. Yet, notwith-

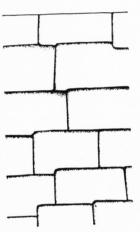

FIG. 26. Inca Wall Construction. It is interesting to note how the stones were cut and fitted into each other.

standing this lack of proper tools, or any instrument in the nature of a derrick to hoist the blocks into position, the old Peruvians have left us walls and immense structures of unsurpassed masonry. In many of these the stones have been so exactly fitted together that it is impossible to insert the blade of a penknife between them. Sometimes the blocks were laid in regular courses. Often they were cut in many angles. One in the Palace of the Inca Rocca, in Cuzco, called by the old historians "La piedra famosa de doce angulos," or "the famous stone of twelve angles," weighs several tons. All its angles fit nicely into or are fitted into by other stones. Squier (435, 437) says:—

The world has nothing to show in the way of stone cutting and fitting to surpass the skill and accuracy displayed in the Inca structures of Cuzco. All modern work of the kind there—and there are some fine examples of skill—looks rude and barbarous in comparison. . . . The Inca architects knew as well how to cut their stones for circular buildings as for rectangular ones. One portion of the Temple of the Sun (Cuzco) is circular, or rather the section of a flattened circle. The stones must have been cut to conform to this shape, for their sides of contact are true radii of the double circle, and the line of general inclination of the wall is perfect in every block.

The Fortress of Sacsahuaman, overlooking Cuzco, is built of irregular blocks of different sizes. It is said to be the grandest specimen of cyclopean masonry in America. One of the stones is twenty-seven feet high, fourteen broad, and twelve feet in thickness.

Architecture. Inca architecture is of a peculiar character; its most striking features are simplicity, symmetry, and solidity. The Incas had no knowledge of the true arch, with its keystone, and did not use columns. Timber was not available in most

FIG. 27. Doorway in a Ruined House, Cuzco. (After E. G. Squier.)

localities where their structures were built. When wood was used no mortise joints were made, and as they did not know the use of iron, the beams were tied together by ropes of vegetable fiber. As just stated, the ancient builders were able to transport bulky masses of porphyry and granite, and cut them with the greatest nicety, but the magnificent walls so raised were roofed with sticks and a thatch of reeds or grass.

The rooms in these buildings had no communication with one another, but generally opened into a court by a doorway, nor had they windows, but were lighted only through their doorways. That these buildings were suited to the character of the climate and were well fitted to resist the terrible earth convulsions that occur repeatedly in that land of volcanoes, is proved by the number which still survive, while many modern structures set up by the Conquerors have toppled over in ruins.

When we turn to details of structure several peculiarities are noted. Thus, Inca architecture is characterized by the form of the door, always much wider at the bottom than at the top (Fig. 27). Again the inner walls of rooms often abound in niches. In describing such niches found in Inca ruins on the Island of Titicaca, Bandelier offers the suggestion that they were used as closets and cupboards. However, other writers look upon them as the recesses in which idols and fetishes were kept.

Roads. Many of the early chroniclers speak of the Inca roads as the greatest achievement of that remarkable people; particularly the road that passes over the great plateau from Cuzco to Quito. For this, galleries had to be cut through the solid rock;

rivers crossed by swinging bridges; precipices
scaled by steps cut into their sides; and ravines
filled up.

Pedro de Cieza (p. 64) says:—

The empire of Peru is so vast, that the Incas ordered a road to be
made, as I have already stated on many occasions, from Chile to
Cuzco, and even from the river Maule as far as the river Angasmayu.

FIG. 28. An Inca Bridge. (After E. G. Squier.)

The rivers mentioned by Pedro de Cieza are near
the southern and northern boundaries of the Inca
Empire, a distance of about 2300 miles. The road
ran between the Cordillera and the coast and crossed
many extensive deserts of shifting sand where no
permanent road could be built, but in such places

stakes were set up as guides to the travelers. When solid ground was reached, a road about fifteen feet wide was leveled and paved with stones. In the first part of Cieza's *Chronicle* he describes a journey he made for the greater part over this coast road, and is continually mentioning that he is on the old Inca road. As nothing has been done to keep these roads in repair since the coming of the Spaniards, only small sections now remain, leading many modern travelers to question that such roads ever existed.

Bridges. Many of the Peruvian rivers run in deep gorges. The roads were carried over these by suspension bridges constructed in the following manner. Two or more, generally four, very stout cables were made of creeping vines or braided withes which were anchored on either side to a pair of heavy stones. Across these cables, at right angles, were laid stout twigs to form a roadway. Two smaller cables were stretched across, several feet above the platform, as hand rails. These supports were necessary as the bridge swung badly during the passage over it (Fig. 28). Hundreds of these bridges are still in use and notwithstanding their unstable appearance are crossed by loaded horses and mules which have largely superseded the llama as beasts of burden in many parts of the country.

Cities and Towns. Such engineering works as we have just cited, suggest a well organized government. The Inca Empire, overthrown by the Spanish invaders, was essentially a city-state, or a country held in military subjection by a single city and its environs. This was the city of Cuzco. Cuzco was then the capital of the Old Inca Empire and the

royal residence and also the Holy City. Here was
the temple of the Sun to which pilgrims resorted
from all parts of the Empire. Prescott says this
temple "was the most magnificent structure in the
New World, and unsurpassed, probably, in the cost-
liness of its decoration by any building in the Old."
(Vol. 1, pp. 35–36.) The present city of Cuzco covers the original site and stands in a valley surrounded by high and snowy mountains. The eleva-
tion of the city is 11,380 feet above the sea, but being
in the tropics enjoys, on the whole, an equable and
salubrious climate. About the *huacapata,* or central
square, now the Plaza Principal, were the twelve
wards of the ancient city. These wards were inhabited by natives of as many principal provinces of the
Empire. The people of each ward wore their distinctive dress which made the city a microcosm of
the Empire.

The royal residence, the Convent of the Virgins of
the Sun, and the homes of the great nobility are described by the old historians as large and imposing
structures. This is borne out by the remains of some
of them, and by the massive fragments of others
that have been incorporated in many of the modern
edifices of Cuzco. Thus, the present church and convent of Santo Domingo occupies the site of the Temple of the Sun, and the illustration in Fig. 29 shows
a portion (on the left) of the old Sun Temple which
has been incorporated in the modern edifice.

On the north side of Cuzco, commanding the city,
is the fortress of Sacsahuaman. We get some idea
of the vast size and strength of this fortress when
told that the wall facing the city is twelve hundred

feet long and of great thickness. All the walls are
of heavy blocks of stone, nicely fitted together without mortar. One of the largest of these stones is
thirty-eight feet long by eighteen broad and six feet
thick (Fig. 4). When we realize that these enor-
mous blocks were hewn from quarries four to fifteen

FIG. 29. The Church and Convent of Santo Domingo, Cuzco. At
the left, may be seen some of the ancient stone work which has been
incorporated into the structure. (After E. G. Squier.)

leagues distant; fashioned and transported across
rivers and over ravines, raised to their elevated
position, and adjusted with the nicest accuracy, our
respect for these ancients increases. Further, this
work was accomplished by a people who had no
knowledge of iron or of machinery such as would be
used by Europeans.

Pachacamac, some twenty miles south, and Ancon, about the same distance north of Lima, and near the seacoast, are familiar names on account of the immense quantity of material in museums from their prehistoric burial grounds. Most of this material was buried many generations before the coming of the Spaniards and the thousands of graves observed testify to a numerous population. Dr. Max Uhle estimates the number of burials to have been between sixty and eighty thousand. The famous temple of Pachacamac, now in ruins, was visited in prehistoric days by native pilgrims from the whole coast of Peru. Here was the shrine of the god, Pachacamac, the chief divinity of the Indians before their conquest by the Inca, who later built a Temple of the Sun, a House of the Virgins near it, but do not appear to have interfered with the religion of the conquered people.

Of Ancon, little can be said, as such structures as once existed there were in complete ruins or had disappeared before the Conquest. It is an interesting fact to archaeologists that the custom of attaching a false head to the mummy bundle was first brought to light by finds in the Necropolis of Ancon. Some remarkably beautiful textiles and pottery, particularly those in the style of Tiahuanaco, have come from the ancient graves of Ancon and Pachacamac (Fig. 17).

The city of Trujillo was founded by Pizarro in 1535, on the site of Chan Chan, the capital and center of the Chimu territory, which extended from near Tumbez on the north to beyond Huaymay on the south. Throughout this stretch of country notable monuments are so numerous and extensive that it will only be possible to give a brief description of a few of them. Squier describes the plain of Chimu as being thickly covered with ruins of the ancient city. They consist of a wilderness of walls, forming great enclosures, each containing a labyrinth of ruined stone dwellings and other edifices, relieved here and there by gigantic *huacas*. These *huacas* or truncated pyramids, are built of compact rubble of broken stones and tenacious clay which forms a hard indurated mass. They are surrounded by high walls of the same material. Obisco *huaca* is 162 feet square and 50 feet high. From another, the *huaca* of Toledo, one Don Garcia Gutierrez, in 1577 and 1578, recovered gold and silver objects to the value of 4,450,784 Spanish dollars. The law was that a fifth of all treasure found belonged to the Crown, and the "Book of Fifths of the Treasury of the Trujillo Municipality" states that Gutierrez presented himself at the royal treasury to deliver a fifth of this sum to the royal chest. There is an old legend that two immense treasures were buried somewhere in Peru. These are known as the *peje grande* or big fish, and the *peje chica* or little fish. The Indians and treasure hunters consider the Gutierrez find to be the little fish, and are still searching for the big fish.

A league from the City of Trujillo are the ruins of a great aqueduct, which tapped the Rio Moche, many miles up towards its source among the mountains, for the water supply of the ancient city. This was carried across the valley on a lofty embankment which is still more than sixty feet high, built of stones and earth with a channel on top.

The Chimu, although nominally at least under the Inca, were flourishing when first discovered by the Spaniards, but Markham says:—

The cruelty of the Spaniards extinguished the Chimu civilization before even a few years have passed. Cieza de Leon tells us of the rapid depopulation of the valleys, and in his time vast tracts were becoming waste for want of people to cultivate the land.

Chapter III

SOCIAL AND POLITICAL ORGANIZATION

WE know far more of the material arts of the Peruvians than we do of their government and social life. The first Europeans to arrive here were fired with a religious zeal to destroy all pagan works and to eliminate all social customs sanctioned by paganism, so it is not strange that our knowledge of native Peruvian life is but fragmentary. It seems, however, that under the régime of the Incas, the country was administered under four subdivisions. Each of these four provinces was under a viceroy or governor, under whom were numerous lesser officers who had jurisdiction over petty offences. There seem to have been few criminal laws, and few were needed by a people who had no money, little trade, and almost nothing that could be called fixed property. Theft, adultery, murder, blasphemy against the Sun, malediction of the Inca, or burning a bridge were punished by death. A rebellious city or province was laid waste and its inhabitants exterminated. Rebellion was an offence against the Child of the Sun and therefore sacrilege.

The land was divided into three parts, one for the Sun, another for the Inca, and the third for the people. The proportion differed in each province. The lands assigned to the Sun furnished a revenue to support the temples and the multitudinous priesthood. The Inca's portion supported the royal establishment and the remainder was divided, per capita, among the people. The tenant's lease of this land expired at the end of the year, and he had no power to alienate or add to his possessions. All lands were cultivated by the people; those belonging to the Sun were attended to first; next came the lands of the old, the sick, widows and orphans, and of soldiers in actual service. The people were then allowed to work their own grounds, and lastly, all joined together, and with many ceremonies cultivated the Inca's portion.

As has already been said, everything in the Empire belonged to the Inca. The mines were wrought exclusively for his benefit. At the time of shearing, the wool was all put in public magazines and, by direction of the Inca, dealt out by officers appointed for that service, to the women of each family to spin and weave into clothing. In like manner cotton was divided. Accounts of these transactions were accurately kept by means of the quipu, a simple device by which any given number could be registered by tying knots in strings. The quipu was also useful in connection with the collection of revenue. Each province was required to furnish a certain proportion of the products grown or manufactured there. The assessment for each locality was regulated by the quantity produced and an inventory was taken every year and the results recorded on knotted strings, which were taken to the capital and submitted to the Inca.

In Book V, Chapter XII, of the Royal Commentaries, Garcilasso says:—

The Policy and Arts which the Incas used in their Conquests, and the manner and methods they pursued in civilizing the People, and reducing them to a course of moral living, is very curious, and worthy to be observed.

He tells us that the Inca never made war without a just cause, but that barbarity and ignorance furnished a sufficient motive.

The first act after a province was conquered was to seize its principal idol as a hostage, and carry it to Cuzco where it was supposed to be held as a prisoner until the conquered people realized that their god had no power to help himself or them, and would be ready to adopt the worship of the Sun, the Inca's god. The Inca had the cacique, his sons, and principal officers brought to Cuzco where they were fêted and treated according to their rank in their own country. They were instructed in the religion, laws, and customs of the Incas, and after a time permitted to return to their people, who were ordered to obey, as formerly, their cacique, as their lord and prince. The Inca caused banquets to be prepared for his new subjects that they might be reconciled with their conquerors. All of which indicates a high order of intelligence and an efficiently organized government.

Inheritance. According to the old chroniclers, if the Inca left no male issue by his legitimate wife, the next of kin succeeded him, provided he was descended from a father and a mother who were both of the blood royal. A son of the Inca by one of his concubines could not inherit. This law was not observed in many of the conquered provinces, where the eldest son, or the one most beloved, or the one most esteemed by the people for qualities that fitted him for the position, must succeed. Differences existed between the laws and civil customs in the countries subjugated by the Incas and their own, because but few changes were required of the conquered people, their internal government remaining untouched, except for the payment of a certain amount of taxes to the Lord of Cuzco. There was, however, enforced recognition of the state religion.

On the other hand, there was no such thing as inheritance of real estate, as all the land belonged to the Inca, who was supposed to allot to each person or each family sufficient for their support, who could not part with any of it, nor could they acquire more from their neighbors.

Army. Such accounts as we have of the number of soldiers in the army of the Inca vary greatly. The most reliable state that the monarch could bring a force of two hundred thousand men into the field. The levies were drawn from all parts of the Empire; more being taken from localities where the people were hardiest than from others. The Inca or one of his nobles of royal blood was in general command, and under him were various officers in command of what we may call battalions and companies.

FIG. 30. Painting on a Pottery Vessel showing a Masked Warrior, Trujillo. In his right hand he carries a warclub, in his left a shield, spears, and throwing stick.

Their arms comprised bows and arrows, long heavy darts which were sometimes thrown with an *atlatl* or throwing stick, a warclub which consisted of a stone or copper star-shaped head and wooden handle, two or three feet in length, and a copper or bronze battle ax. For fighting in open country the sling was an effective weapon, as a stone could be thrown with it with great accuracy. For defensive armor, they carried a shield, and some-

times wore a poncho of quilted cotton much like that
of the ancient Mexicans.

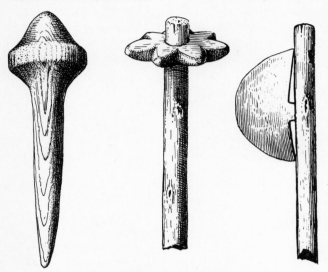

FIG. 31.   Warclubs and a Battle Ax.

The uniqueness of
the *atlatl,* or throw-
ing stick, may justify
further comment. In
numerous hunting and
war scenes painted on
pottery vessels, men
are represented in the
act of throwing spears
or heavy darts with
this instrument. This
device practically ex-
tends the length of the

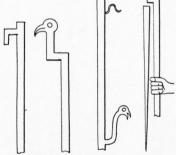

FIG. 32.   Forms of Throwing
Sticks used in Peru. Drawn from
examples depicted on pottery vessels.

arm and the spear is discharged with much greater force. It is, however, a very simple affair; a stick with a projection at the distal end, against which the butt end of the spear rests when being thrown. Fig. 32 shows several forms of Peruvian *atlatls*. In still another form represented, a cord takes the

FIG. 33

FIG. 34

FIG. 33. Killing a Deer with a Lance and Throwing Stick.

FIG. 34. A Deer Hunting Scene on a Water Vessel. The deer have been driven into a net, where they are being killed with clubs and heavy darts. Here a metal hook and cord is used instead of the usual spear thrower.

place of a stick. This cord had on one end a hook, probably of copper, against which the spear rested. The other end was wound about the fingers, while the thumb and first finger held the spear. The use of the *atlatl* in hunting is shown in Fig. 33.

Magazines filled with grain, mostly maize, were scattered all over the country for the use of the army. Pizarro often fed his followers for a considerable time by robbing these storehouses.

FIG. 35. Pottery Vessel showing Manner of Carrying Burdens, supported by a Forehead Strap.

We are told that the standing army of the Inca was not large, but that additional troops could be mobilized in a very short time, through an admirable system of runners. The command having been

given, a runner started at top speed for the next
post, and delivered the message, which the second
man carried to the third, and so on. These posts
were but a few miles apart and a runner was always
stationed on duty at each of them.

Transportation. No such military operations as
we have described could be maintained without ade-
quate transportation facilities. Yet, the prehistoric
methods were simple and primitive. For example,
the greater part of transportation today, as it was
before the Conquest, is on the back of the Indian, the
load being supported by a strap which passes over
the forehead or around the chest. The only beast of
burden possessed by the prehistoric Peruvians was
the llama. This animal can carry a load of 100
pounds, a distance of ten or twelve miles a day. In
present-day Peru it is common to see many llamas
with their loads marching in single file over the
mountain trails, in charge of their Indian *arieros,* or
drivers. Presumably it was thus in prehistoric
times.

On the water, the balsa, a curious raft-like boat,
was and still is used. In constructing this boat or
raft, cigar-shaped bundles of rushes are tied together. Two or three of these bundles are bound
together with the front end turned up, something
after the fashion of a gondola. The balsa is very
buoyant at first, but after a time, becomes water-
logged and must be taken from the water and dried
in the sun. Some of the larger ones were fitted with
a mast and a sail made of rushes.

All accounts agree that when the Inca, Atahualpa,
went to meet the Spaniards in the great plaza at
Cajamarca he was carried in a sedan by his atten-

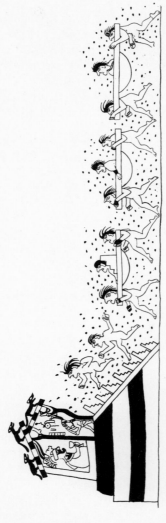

FIG. 36. Paying Homage to the Inca. From painting on a pottery vessel from Trujillo. At the left we see the Inca in a house built on terraces. Two runners mount the terraces followed by a man who, judging from his throne-like sedan, is the chief of some conquered tribe. The second man is evidently inferior in rank to the first, as he rides in a plain sedan, while the third man has a rope around his neck, indicating that his position was lower still.

69

dants. Historians say this sedan was decorated with feathers and large plates of gold and silver. The men who carried the Inca were especially trained for this work. Other carriers were always beside them to catch the pole in case one stumbled or fell. Such an accident would cost the bearer his life.

These sedans were used by others beside the Inca, as is shown in Fig. 36. This drawing is from a pottery water vessel from Trujillo and it tells quite a story. At the left we see the Inca in a house built on terraces (indicated by the step form figures). Two runners mount the terraces followed by a man who, judging from his throne-like sedan, seems to be the chief of some conquered tribe. The second man is evidently inferior in rank to the first, as he rides in a plain sedan; the third man has a rope around his neck, indicating that his position was inferior to the other two.

FIG. 37. Figure of a Warrior on a Prehistoric Shawl-like Garment from Ica, Peru. (Nazca Culture.) The warrior carries two human heads, as trophies, and a warclub.

War Trophies. All barbaric peoples collect gruesome trophies from the battlefield and the Peruvians were no exception. The prehistoric people of Nazca preserved the heads of their enemies as trophies of war. Fig. 37 shows a design on a shawl-like garment from an ancient grave. The decoration is in embroidery, done with a thorn or copper needle. Each figure carries a pole on which hang two of these human heads.

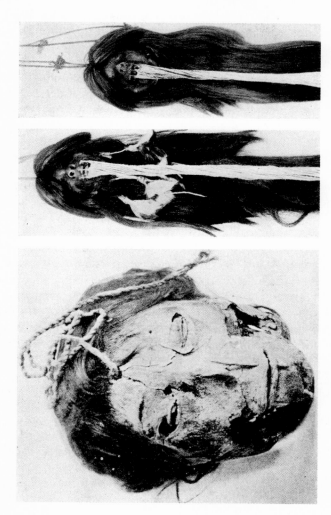

FIG. 38. War Trophies. *a*, Human head, from Nazca, Peru; *b*, Shrunken human heads from the Jivaros Indians of Eastern Ecuador.

71

Dr. Julio Tello has made a special study of such examples of these preserved heads as are found in museum collections, and the process of making them, according to him, is as follows. After the skin has been taken off the whole or part of the occiput is removed, the foramen magnum enlarged, and all the soft parts taken out. Then, a perforation is made in the frontal bone close to the hair of the head. Through this perforation a cord is passed, and a cross piece of wood is tied to the inner end to prevent its pulling out. The orbits and all cavities are filled with cotton, and the skin replaced. Generally two sticks are passed up through the lips (Fig. 38a).

The shrunken heads made by the wild Jivaros Indians are familiar objects in museums. These Indians, who are now divided into a number of small groups, are located in the eastern part of Ecuador. The present Jivaros are as ardent head hunters as were their ancestors many centuries ago. The standing of a man in the tribe depended on his courage and ability as a warrior, as shown by the number of the tribal enemies he had killed. The possession of these heads (war trophies) would be accepted as proof of his prowess (Fig. 38b).

The details of preparing these ghastly trophies are as follows: After the head is severed from the body a cut is made from the base of the skull down through the skin of the neck. Through the opening thus made the bones of the head are carefully removed; the skin and remaining soft parts are dipped into the juice of the *huito* fruit, which stains them black. The skin is now ready for the shrinking process. In some Jivaro groups a number of hot stones are put into the skin which is constantly

turned in order to bring them in contact with all
parts of it. In other localities a single stone, nearly
the size of the head, is first used, then a smaller one,
and so on until the skin is reduced to the desired
size, usually that of a small orange. In still other
localities, hot sand takes the place of stones. Long
pendent cords fasten the lips together, and one is
run through the top of the head by which it is sus-
pended. The cut in the back of the neck is then
sewed up and the trophy is finished.

As soon as the Jivaros learned that these
shrunken heads were in demand by white men, as
curiosities, they began to prepare them for traders,
who usually carried them down the Amazon to Para
where they found a ready market for them. After
this, the Indians were by no means particular as to
whether the head was that of a friend or an enemy.
So even in early times Peru and other South American countries passed laws with severe penalties for
any one who was known to have prepared these
heads, but it is difficult to reach the transgressors,
and nothing has been accomplished towards stopping the practice.

We have gone into this detail regarding a modern
practice, because there seems to have been some historical connection between the trophies of the old
Peruvians and these modern savages.

Peruvian Women. The traditional manner of
judging a people is to note the status of their women.
At least, knowledge of the woman's lot in Peru, will
give some idea of the social life of the time. So,
from the old chroniclers we learn that the women,
when not employed in necessary household work, or
in planting or gathering crops, were engaged in

spinning and weaving.   On visits to neighbors, or
on journeys, they carried a supply of cotton or wool

FIG. 39.   A Modern Peruvian Woman from Puno, spinning Yarn
as She walks along the Street.   She carries her sleeping mat of reeds
on her back.

and their spindles, and spun as they walked along.
Each one had to weave enough cloth for herself and
her family.

Conditions have not changed much, since it is a
common occurrence to see a present day Peruvian

Indian woman spinning as she walks. She generally carries some burden, perhaps a jar of water or a reed sleeping mat on her back, held by a strap passing over the forehead or around the chest, while her hands are employed in spinning. We cannot be sure as to the methods of spinning in prehistoric time, but the later Spanish accounts of contemporary methods state that the material to be spun was sometimes carried on a distaff, but more usually in a cone-shaped bundle, under the left arm. A certain amount was first drawn out and both hands were used to clear it of any irregularities, and to reduce it to the desired thickness. It was then attached to the spindle by a slip knot, so that the spindle could be recovered after being twirled between the thumb and forefinger of the right hand, and allowed to drop. The spindle, revolving rapidly as it fell, gave the proper twist to the thread. This reads very much like the European way of spinning.

When a woman in the common rank of life visited a *Palla,* a woman of the royal blood, she did not carry her spinning with her, but asked for some work to do. This showed that she did not come as an equal, but to pay her respects to a superior. The *Palla* was usually courteous enough to allow her to help in the work in which she or her daughters were engaged. This was a great compliment as it implied that the visitor was on a social level with her hostess. To have allowed the visitor to assist the servants in their work would have been considered as ranking her with them.

Garcilasso (Chap. XIV) says:—

The Spanish women which came afterwards to live in Cuzco imitated this custom, after the manner of the Indian women, carrying

always their work whensoever they came to make their visits; and
this fashion was in use amongst them to their great commendation
until such time as Francisco Hernandez began his civil war, which
as it introduced nothing but tyranny and cruelty, so it abolished this
laudable custom, and discountenanced all virtuous and innocent
practices.

Garments with holes, either from wear or from
fire, were not patched, but were put into a loom and
yarns of the color originally used in the cloth were
woven in. To repair a simple tear, the edges were
sewed together with thorn or copper needles. In
the Museum collections are several ponchos that
have undergone such repairs.

The women partook in all public assemblies, religious or otherwise, and to them fell the labor of preparing the large amount of corn beer (*chicha*) drunk
on these occasions. Whatever the nature of the as-
sembly, it always resolved itself into what Cieza de
Leon called drinking bouts. This is true of all
Indian gatherings today; both men and women generally continue drumming, singing, dancing, and
drinking until completely intoxicated, or until the
supply of *chicha* is exhausted.

E. G. Squier was at Tiahuanaco, in 1875, during
the celebrations of the potato festival and of Corpus
Christi, which took place at the same time. His description of these ceremonies presents a vivid picture of Indian gatherings at that time. He says:—

Each group danced vigorously to its united music, which made up
in volume what it lacked in melody—wild and piercing, yet lugu-
brious; the shrill pipe and dull drum, with frequent blasts on cow's
horns by amateurs among the spectators, filled the ear with discordant
sounds. Every man seemed anxious to excel his neighbor in the energy
of his movements which were often extravagant; but the motions of
the women were slow and stately. The music had its cadences, and its

emphatic parts were marked by corresponding emphatic movements in the dance. The ''devilish music'' that Cortez heard after his first repulse before Mexico, lasting the livelong night, and which curdled his blood with horror, while his captured companions were sacrificed to Huitzlipochtli, the Aztec war god, could not be stranger or more fascinating, more weird or savage, than that which rung in our ears during the rest of our stay in Tiahuanuco. All night and all day, still the festival went on, growing wilder and noisier, and only culminating when the feast of the Church commenced. It was an extraordinary spectacle, that of the symbols of Christianity and the figures of our Saviour and the saints carried by a reeling priest and staggering Indians through the streets of Tiahuanuco, while the *Chuño* (potato) revellers danced and drummed around them. . . . We left the scene with a clear conviction that the savage rites of the Aymaras had changed in name only, and that the festival we had witnessed was a substantial rehearsal of ceremonies and observances antedating the Discovery (pp. 306–307).

We are told that on the death of an Inca, or great chieftain, his wives and favorite women struggled for the privilege of burial with him, that they might accompany him into the other world and continue their services in the other life. Cieza de Leon says that more than 4,000 souls, women, pages, and other servants, together with immense riches were buried in the tomb with the Inca, Huayna Capac. The following quotation is from the same authority, but must be taken with the proverbial grain of salt.

As soon as Huayna Capac was dead the lamentations were so great that the shouting rose up to the clouds, and the noise so stupefied the birds that they fell from a great height to the ground. (Chronicles of Peru, Second Part, p. 222.)

As the women were always the chief mourners on such occasions Cieza pays a great compliment to the strength of their voices.

Chapter IV

RELIGION AND CEREMONIES

WE come now to the most interesting aspect of ancient Peruvian life, but one concerning which our knowledge leaves much to be desired. That these people had a highly complex system of philosophy and beliefs is obvious, it is also clear that their ritualistic ceremonies were elaborate and that there was an official priesthood. Thus, from the accounts of the early Spanish writers, such as Blas Valera, Cieza de Leon, Molina, and Garcilasso, we learn that the Inca were Sun worshipers, but that they worshiped numerous minor deities, the Moon, the sister-wife of the Sun, Venus as the page of the Sun, Thunder and Lightning as his dread ministers, and the Rainbow as a beautiful emanation of the deity. The Coast peoples worshiped the Sea; and the fish, being the natural emblem of the sea, it is no wonder that we find so many of the works in stone and textiles decorated with various fish forms. The evil god, or personification of sin, they called *supay*. But the peoples of the coast and of the highlands held in veneration a great variety of idols and charms, concerning which Acosta (p. 339) quaintly says:—

The Devil has not been contented to make these blind Indians to worship the Sun, Moon, Stars, earth and sea, and many other general things in nature, but he hath passed on further, giving them for God, and making them subject to base and abject things.

Where maize grew, every household had its *Sara mana* which represented the spiritual essence of the maize, to which prayers were offered. Vessels ornamented with ears of corn will be found in every large

Peruvian collection, and it is natural to assume that these are for the most part household idols.

Again, the so-called Llama Mana in stone, wood, or pottery is the figure of a llama with a cavity in its back. An offering, in the form of grains of corn, or coca leaves, was placed in the cavity and the figure buried in the field where the llamas grazed, as a prayer for the increase of the flock.

Then, each family, and for the most part, every person, had a number of sacred objects, called *conopas*. Those belonging exclusively to the individual were buried with him at death. These were any small object that took his fancy. Thus, long after the advent of the Spaniards, if an Indian found an odd-shaped pebble, particularly if it bore some resemblance to some familiar animal form, he would often take it to the priest and ask if it were a *huaca,* or a holy object. If the priest answered yes, it was carefully preserved as his personal *conopa.*

Among the religious buildings of the Peruvians were the temples for the Virgins of the Sun. The inmates of these institutions, or convents, were girls taken from their homes at a very tender age and their lives dedicated to the service of their deity, the Sun. They were under the care of the *mamaconas,* or elderly matrons, who instructed them in the nature of their religious duties, and in spinning and weaving. In fact, their chief occupation seems to have been the making of fine garments of vicuña wool for the Inca and his family. Specializing in this work all their lives, they naturally became very expert weavers, and doubtless we are indebted to them for many of the best specimens shown in the textile cases. It is also well to note that the motive back of their excellence was religious.

Chastity and purity in life was the motto of these institutions, and any transgression by an inmate was punished by burying her alive. Her lover was strangled, and the village to which he belonged was razed to the ground. These maidens were considered as spiritual brides of the Sun, and the Inca, being the son of the Sun, and his representative on earth was allowed to choose his concubines from among them. When he tired of them they were sent to their homes, and abundant provision made for them. Then they passed the remainder of their lives in great state, universally reverenced as brides of the Inca. They could never marry, as it would be profane for the wife of the Inca to own any other husband.

The above describes these institutions in general, but there seems to have been a convent at Cuzco with a different order of nuns. These virgins were carefully selected as to their lineage; both father and mother were of pure royal blood, and they were never accepted if over eight years of age. These selected virgins were espoused to the Sun, and it was believed he would have children by them. No outsider, man or woman, was allowed to enter the convent with the exception of the queen, through whom they made their wants known to the Inca.

Such accounts as we have concerning the religion of the Peruvian coast peoples before the Inca conquest, are very unreliable. It appears that their chief divinity was Pachacamac, the creator of the world. His shrine was in the temple at Pachacamac, about twenty miles south of Lima, in the valley of the Lurin, and only a short distance from the present small town of Pachacamac. From all parts of the coast the Indians came to worship at this shrine, for it was to them what Mecca is to the Mohammedan world. When the Incas conquered the country they built a large Temple of the Sun, and House of the Virgins of the Sun side by side with the Temple of Pachacamac, but it does not appear that they suppressed or in any way interfered with the ancient worship of Pachacamac.

Pizarro early heard stories of the immense wealth in this old temple of Pachacamac, and after he had taken Atahualpa prisoner, he sent his brother, Hernandez, from Cajamarca to seize the treasures reported to exist there. Hernandez caused the vault in which the idol was kept to be destroyed, and the idol to be broken into pieces. It is reported that he secured a large amount of gold and silver.

Ceremonies and Festivals. The most magnificent religious festival of the Inca period was held at the time of the summer solstice. Indian nobles gathered in Cuzco from all parts of the empire. The people had fasted for three days previous, and no fire was allowed to be lighted in the houses. At the appointed time, the Inca arrived, followed by the whole population of the city. All were dressed in their gayest garments, the noblest vying with each other in the display of ornaments and gaudy featherwork. They watched impatiently for the rising of their deity, the sun, and as his first rays were seen, a great shout broke forth from the multitude, accompanied by songs and barbaric instruments. After various ceremonies of adoration, the Inca offered a libation to the sun from a large golden vase filled with the fermented liquor made of maize. He then drank from the vase himself, and gave what remained to his royal kindred. This ceremony over, they all went in order of procession toward the Coricancha.

As they entered the street leading to this sacred edifice, all except the Inca removed their sandals, and this he did before passing through the portals of the temple. After the ceremonies in the temple, the high priest offered a sacrifice, generally a llama. He opened the body, and sought, from the appearance which it exhibited, to read the future.

Sacrifices. All accounts agree that the Incas held a great festival once a year, in Cuzco, where all the idols were assembled, some from a considerable distance. They were accompanied by the priests who had charge of them. There were present the Inca with his *Orejones,* the principal men of the city, and a multitude of men and women from all over the empire. The object of this meeting was to obtain forecasts of the coming year from the idols, whose answers to the questions put to them were delivered by the priests. The questions asked of the idols were whether the Inca would have a long life; whether or not the crops would be abundant; if enemies would come, and if so, from what direction. Many young llamas and guinea pigs were sacrificed before the idols were consulted. The Incas did not sacrifice human life. On these occasions the *Orejones* inaugurated a succession of festivals and drinking bouts for which the Virgins of the Sun had prepared an immense amount of *chicha,* their favorite intoxicating beverage.

Further descriptive details concerning this and other ceremonies will be found in the special works listed in the bibliography.

Folk Customs and Mythology. Under this head will be given information as to the social procedures and folk customs best known to us and while they are extremely fragmentary, they will nevertheless give a general idea of this phase of native culture. As in other parts of the world every important act was in conformity to a ritual. Thus, when the earth had been prepared for planting, the people sang certain songs. The substance of these songs was taken from the word *hayllis,* which means triumph, as if they triumphed over the earth and took fruit from it. Also, among the highland people a festival was held when the corn first appeared above ground. At this time sacrifices of young llamas were offered and the deity petitioned not to allow the crops to be destroyed by frost.

Garcilasso de la Vega has given us descriptions of many of these festivals, among which is that of one held when a great plague, which had killed many people, came to an end. This always took place on the fifth day of the moon, after the equinox in September. For several days previous the people ate but little. The women prepared a certain kind of bread, moistened with blood, and but half baked. During the night, those who had fasted applied some of this bread to their heads, mouths, breasts, shoulders, arms and legs, believing that by so doing they had cleansed their bodies of all infirmities. Bread was then applied to walls of the houses as a ceremony of purification.

As soon as the sun rose the people prayed to it to deliver the city from all calamities. Presently an Inca, of the royal blood, appeared. He was elegantly dressed and bore a lance in his hand. He ran to the market place, where four other Incas, each carrying a lance, met him. The messenger, on meeting the four Incas, touched the heads of their lances with his, told them that the sun commanded them to purify and cleanse the city of all infirmities and diseases, and gave them the power to do it.

Garcilasso has given us some account of the ancient marriage ceremonies:—

It will now be proper for us to treat of their marriages, and how they were joined together in the kingdoms and provinces subjected to the Inca. In order hereunto it is to be noted that every year, or every two years, the king commanded his officers to take an account of such young men and maidens, of his lineage, as were marriageable within the city of Cuzco, that so they might be matched together: the maidens were to be of eighteen to twenty years of age, and the young men from twenty to twenty-four and upwards; under that age they were not esteemed to be of years of consent, for that it was necessary they should be of a ripe age and judgment to govern their families.

At the ceremonies of matrimony the Inca stood between the two persons, and casting his eyes upon them both, he called the man by his name, and then the woman, and taking their hands into his, joined them together, which being the bond of matrimony, the function was performed. They went to the house of the bridegroom's father, where the wedding was kept for four or six days with great rejoycing.

The next day officers appointed for the purpose performed the marriage ceremony in other localities.

There was even a ceremony at the weaning of children, according to Garcilasso. This took place when the child was two or more years old. First the hair of its head was cut off with flints, and a name

given to it. After the god-
father had cut off a lock, the
rest of the kindred did the
same, in order of their age and
rank. All taking part in the
ceremony brought a present
for the child. Drink was then
brought in, and singing, dancing, and drinking were con-
tinued for three or four days.

Of mythological characters
they had many. Three of these
are frequently represented on
the textiles and pottery of the
time. A figure, part man and
part puma, is called the puma
god. We know also that they
worshiped the puma. A being
part man and part fish is
known as the fish god. The

FIG. 40. Mythological
Beings: Puma, Fish, and
Bird Gods.

inhabitants on the coast worshiped the sea; the fish
was the natural emblem of the sea and was much
used as a decorative motive. Another being, part
man and part bird, is called the condor god.

Examples of these gods are shown in Fig. 40.
Each has human arms and legs, and the kind of animal combined with man is easily recognizable. The
raised back and tail of the puma, the fins of the fish,
and the feathers in the wing and tail of the bird
identify them. Of course, all parts are highly conventionalized. The puma god in Fig. 40 is from
Nazca pottery and wears a face mask as do most figures in the art of that locality. However, it must
not be understood that these gods were always rep-

resented exactly as shown here, for in different localities the conventionalization of the same form varied.

It is a curious fact that in the folklore of many primitive peoples of South America there are at the present time, or have been in the past, mythological fables that resemble the Biblical accounts of the great flood and of the virgin birth. A Peruvian account of virgin birth was recorded by Francisco Avila, the cura of San Damian, in the province of Huarochiri, Peru, in 1608, which runs as follows:—

The god, Uira-cocha caused the virgin goddess, Cavillaca, to conceive by dropping before her the fruit from a lucuma tree. To her own astonishment she gave birth to a son. She assembled all the gods to find out who was the father, by the test of the child recognizing them. Uira-cocha came disguised as a wretched beggar. The child went at once to him. Cavillaca was so ashamed and enraged at the thought of such a character being considered the father of her boy that she snatched up the child and fled to the sea. Uira-cocha resumed his godlike form and pursued her, calling to her to turn back and look at him. She was soon out of sight, and when she reached the shore of Pachacamac she entered the sea with her child, and immediately both were transformed into two rocky islets, which may still be seen.

The Inca variant of the story of the great flood, as given by Christoval de Molina, was written between 1570 and 1584. Molina was priest of the hospital for natives at Cuzco and was a master of the Quechua language. His statement is as follows:

In the life of Manco Ccapac, who was the first Inca, and from whom they began to be called the children of the Sun, and to worship the Sun, they had a full account of the deluge. They say that all people and all created things perished in it, insomuch that the water rose above all the highest mountains in the world. No living things survived, except a man and a woman, who remained in a box, and when the waters subsided, the wind carried them to Huanaco.

If we attempt to go much deeper into the mythology of the Peruvians, through the writings of the early Spanish historians, we encounter little but contradictory statements, and make no progress. This seems to have been the opinion of Paul Rycaut, who says (1568) in the introduction to his translation of *The Royal Commentaries* of Peru by Garcilasso de la Vega:—

However, being, as our author says, delivered by tradition, and commonly believed amongst their people of the better degree, it may contain divers truths mixed with abundance of fictions and foolish inventions.

As has been stated before, the religion of the Inca period centered around Lake Titicaca. Thus, according to a tradition of the Incas, the children of the Sun, Manco Ccapac, and Mama Ocllo, his wife, who was also his sister, were sent from the sacred Island of Titicaca to instruct the savage tribes who inhabited the country, in religion and the arts. Manco was given a golden wedge and told to establish his capital city wherever it should leave his hand and sink into the earth. They traveled northward along the western shore of Lake Titicaca, and still northward, until they reached the site of the present city of Cuzco, when the wedge sank into the earth. Here they settled and began teaching the savages to worship the sun. Manco also taught the men how to cultivate the earth, to hunt, and to catch fish; and

Mama Ocllo taught the women to spin and weave. And here, in time, arose the capital of the Inca empire.

Another account of the founding of Cuzco is to be found in the Poccari-Tampu myth. Tampu-Tocco was supposed to be a hill with three openings or windows. The legend runs that a tribe emerged from one of the windows and from the central one, four august men with their wives. The four men were children of the Sun, and they decided to seek more fertile regions, thinking no doubt that with the help of the tribe they could conquer the savages and take possession of the country. They traveled slowly, even stopping to plant crops and harvest them; but being always dissatisfied with the locality they moved from time to time.

During the migration, Manco contrived, in some way, to get rid of his three brothers, and so become sole leader. After many years they reached Mata-hua, at the edge of Cuzco Valley. From here Manco hurled his golden staff as far as Huanay-pata, where it sank into the earth, and there he founded the city of Cuzco.

Burial Customs. In the burials of the dead we find that much the same distinction obtained then as now. The bodies of the wealthy were wrapped in many pieces of beautiful tapestry, and if that of a man, in the grave beside him were placed his implements used in war, hunting, and fishing; also a number of the finest pottery vessels, and sometimes objects of gold and silver. With these an abundant supply of food, coca leaves, and *chicha* (a beer made from maize) were left near the body. The body of a poor man was thrust into a hole in the nitrous sand

Fɪɢ. 41. Mummy Bundle with a False Head, from a grave at Santa Rosa, fourteen miles from Ancon. Attached to the bundle are dolls, cloth bags, and sticks wound with colored yarns. The false head has eyes, nose, mouth, and forehead ornaments of silver. The true head is in the bundle.

of the coast, or into a crevice of the rocks in the mountains. His vestments were poor and mean, as his friends could supply none better. Beside him, we generally find an ear of corn, a gourd or pottery vessel for water, and often a few odd-shaped stones, his amulets or charms (Fig. 41).

In the coast region, particularly at Pachacamac, the dessicated bodies, generally called mummies, are often found in little adobe vaults which are covered with sticks and a layer of rushes. The bodies are in a sitting position, the knees drawn up, and the head

a b
FIG. 42. Burial Towers. a, Acora; b, Sillustani.

resting upon them. With the body of a woman is generally found her work basket (see Fig. 14). In some localities a false head was attached to the mummy bundle. The significance of this custom is unknown.

At Sillustani and Acora, in Peru, in the Collao, a part of the Titicaca basin, and in a number of localities in Bolivia, hundreds of burial towers may be seen. Some are still in perfect condition, but the greater part are more or less in ruins, having been shaken down by earthquakes or demolished by treasure hunters. They vary in shape, some are quadrangular, and others are in the form of an inverted truncated cone. On the rocky peninsula of Sillustani, which extends out into the lake of Umayo are many of these Chullpas, and hundreds more of the ruins of these structures can be seen on the neighboring hills. One of the largest and best preserved towers on this peninsula (Fig. 42b) is in the form of an inverted truncated cone, thirty-nine feet high, sixteen feet in diameter at the base, increasing, until at the spring of the dome, the diameter is eighteen feet and ten inches. It is built of admirably cut and fitted blocks of hard basalt. The entrance, just large enough to admit the body of a man, is cut through a solid block. The vault inside is ten feet in diameter and twelve feet high with an opening leading into a small chamber above.

There has been much speculation as to how the ancient Peruvians managed to raise immense stones into position in many of their structures. The answer is found on the peninsula of Sillustani, and I give it in the words of E. G. Squier, who says:—

Some of the unfinished Chullpas enlighten us as to the manner in which their builders, and those of other Peruvian monuments, contrived to raise heavy stones to considerable heights without the aid of derricks and pulleys. We find, built up against the Chullpa, inclined planes of stone and earth, up which the stones were moved, probably with levers, and possibly with the aid of rollers. As the structure rose in height the plane was raised accordingly; and when the structure was finished, the plane was dug away (pp. 380–381).

It is altogether probable that the great Pyramids of Egypt were built in this same way.

CHAPTER V

DECORATIVE AND RELIGIOUS ART

WE have taken note of the architecture and metal work of Peru, and since sculpture in stone was not well developed, except in a very few localities, there remain only textiles and pottery to be discussed under the head of art. The decorations of cloth and pottery were carried to a level of excellence rarely reached by any people. In viewing museum collections, one observes that the types of designs are the same whether upon pottery or cloth, and that for the most part there are but four motives: the human figure, the bird, the fish, and the puma. Sometimes we find realistic representations of these forms, but in the majority of cases they are more or less conventionalized. Often these are so far degenerated as to be recognized only by one familiar with the art motives, and this may proceed until only a geometrical figure remains. What has been said about the prevalence of these four motives applies more particularly to the decorations of the pre-Inca people whose works constitute the greater part of most Peruvian collections. About Cuzco, before the Incas had extended their reign over other sections of the country, the pottery was generally sober in color, decorated, in the main, with geometric designs and depending for beauty on form and line. Later, the Incas adopted some of the anthropomorphic forms of the older peoples. The older Peruvians represented their gods and various mythological beings by combining parts of the human figure with those of some animal.

FIG. 43. Conventionalization in Ancient Peruvian Art.

93

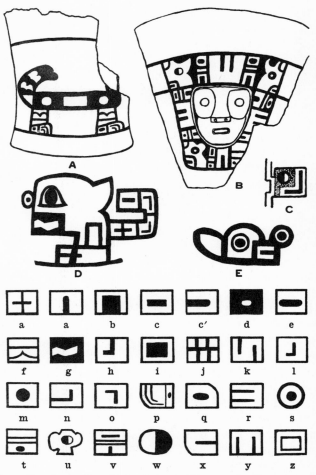

FIG. 44. Conventionalized Animal Figures in Peruvian Art. Those on the lower half of the plate and similar figures have frequently been mistaken for hieroglyphs.

We have treated Peruvian art at some length in another place, making it unnecessary to give an extended account here; but a few examples of their conventionalized figures will not be out of place (see Fig. 43). These black and white drawings give us only forms, and no suggestion of the color schemes which constitute their beauty.

Fig. 44 deals with the curious glyph-like figures so common on pottery vessels from the Island of Titicaca, Copacabana, and Tiahuanaco. While many of these figures might easily be mistaken for hieroglyphs we shall see that most, if not all of them, are parts of conventionalized animal forms, or the markings on such forms. Several of these designs are usually grouped together on a vessel without any observable relationship; sometimes they are turned one way and sometimes another.

Beginning at the upper left hand corner of Fig. 44, the first is a broken kero or cup of terra cotta from Tiahuanaco. The puma figure has on its legs the same markings as will be found in Fig. 44f, and the feet as in Fig. 44p. These two figures make clear my meaning when I said above that they were sometimes turned one way and sometimes another.

The second is a large painted potsherd from Tiahuanaco. It will be seen that quite a number of the glyph-like figures are depicted on it. On the upper curved line of decorations are two llama heads. The one on the extreme left shows a part of the ring nose (Fig. 44s), the divided eye (Fig. 44w), and the form of mouth shown in Fig. 44x. The llama on the right has the ordinary form of eye. Another llama head is seen on the lower line to the left.

The third (Fig. 44c) is a puma head on a woven fabric from Pachacamac. The divided eye is like Fig. 44w and this way of representing the mouth will be found in Fig. 44l.

The fourth is a puma figure painted on a clay cup from the Island of Titicaca. Its ring nose is like Fig. 44s, its mouth like Fig. 44g, and the four designs on the tail will be found in Figs. 44a, e, l, o.

The fifth, is from a painted cup, Copacabana. The mouth is shown in Fig. 44a', c', the eye and nose in Fig. 44s. While studying the various conventionalized animal figures I have noticed that the eye is often represented as in Fig. 44d, i, m, s, w. and z; the mouth as in Figs. 44a', c', g, h, j, l, n, o, z; the ear as in Fig. 44k; and the feet as in Fig. 44p. Spots on the tips of feathers are shown as in Figs. 44c, d, e, i, m, and z.

These glyph-like figures were copied from decorations on pottery vessels, but they are also common to the textile fabrics, as we should expect to be the case where freehand drawings were copied in woven designs, and woven figures, with step form lines from the technique of weaving, were in turn copied in decorations on pottery vessels.

Music and Dancing. Instruments of percussion included the drum, bell, rattles, and large shells used as a cymbal. The wind instruments were the pan-pipe or syrinx, end-blown flute, resonator whistles, trumpets of clay and shell, a great variety of simple whistles, and the double whistling jar (Fig. 45).

These double whistling jars are a rather curious invention. They consist of two pottery vessels connected near the bottom in such a way that water passes freely from one to the other. Near the top of

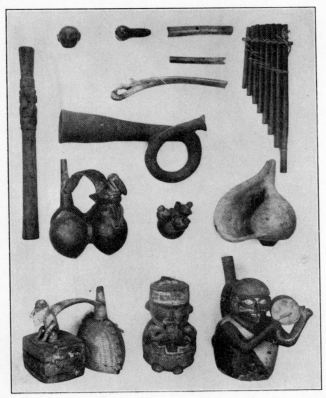

FIG. 45. Musical Instruments: Flutes, panpipe, trumpets of wood, clay, and shell; double whistling jars, and human figures in clay, playing a panpipe and a drum.

97

FIG. 46. A Double Whistling Jar.

FIG. 47. A Circular Gold Ornament, showing the Use of the
Trumpet. The upper one at the left is of shell; the lower, is of
terra cotta.

98

the front or first jar (usually surmounted by a human or animal figure) is the opening of the whistle. When the jars have been partly filled and are swung backward and forward, a series of whistling sounds is produced. As the vessel swings forward and upward, the water is lowered in the first jar and raised in the other; in the backward motion it rushes back into the first, forcing the air out through the whistle.

It has often been said that the sound emitted by these jars resembles the cry of the animal repre-

FIG. 48.   Dancing Figures modeled in Relief on Two Pottery Vessels. The musical instruments played by the dancers are the flute, panpipe, and small drums. In the lower figure may be seen jars of *chicha*, a fermented drink made of maize.

sented on the vessel. A careful examination of more than eighty of them leads to the conclusion that this is the result of a lively imagination, and that they are whistles pure and simple.

We have many representations on pottery of the manner of dancing which does not seem to have changed up to 1649, when Alonso de Ovalle wrote this quaint account:—

Their way of dancing is with little jumps, and a step or two, not rising much from the ground, and without any capers such as the Spanish use; they dance all together in a ring. (p. 122.)

The first and simplest element of music is rhythm. In singing or dancing a desire for some sound that shall clearly mark rhythm is universal; hence, the drum was undoubtedly the most important instrument used in dances. In the representations left us (see Fig. 48) some of the dancers are shown playing the panpipe and the end-blown flute. From what we know of these wind instruments it is very improbable that any attempt was made to play any tune in unison, but each player made all the noise he could.

In 1895 Bandelier thus described an Indian dance on the Island of Titicaca (p. 117) :—

Within a very short time the courtyard was filled with dancers, with or without official costume, and with the same din and uproar, though proportionally less than at other places and larger gatherings. The wonted disregard for symmetry and harmony prevailed, showing that discordant noise and irregular motions are inherent to most aboriginal dances of Bolivia.

CHAPTER VI

ACHIEVEMENTS IN CULTURE

IT is always difficult to form a satisfactory esti-
mate of a civilization, even when it is contemporary with our own, but when as in the case of the
Peruvians, all we have are archaeological collections
supplemented by fragmentary documentary data,
the difficulty is greatly increased. Nevertheless, it
is possible to show that Peruvian culture was on a
high level, by noting the knowledge of astronomy,
mathematics, etc.

Astronomy. While we know that the Incas understood something of astronomy, their knowledge
fell short of that of the Mexicans and Central Amer-
icans who devised a remarkably correct calendar.
Yet, many of the early chroniclers state that the Incas determined the length of the solar year and the
periods of the solstices by noting shadows cast by
specially constructed towers and taking observations
between them. They called the sun, *Ynti;* the moon,
Quilla; Venus, *Chasca;* and the year, *Huata.* Time
was generally reckoned by moons.

Garcilasso says there were sixteen of these towers
at Cuzco, eight to the east, and eight to the west of
the city. Acosta gives the number as twelve, and
Betanzos as four. The latter call them pyramids.
Such structures they called *Inti-huatana,* which was
equivalent to the place where the Sun was tied up.
Squier describes the *Inti-huatana* at Pisac at some
length, and says that such structures seem to have
always been formed out of a rock by making its top
level, leaving only a projecting cone in its center.
He says (p. 529) :—

Making due allowance for the probable exaggerations and misinformation of Garcilasso, we may readily believe that the towers of which he speaks—the pillars mentioned by Acosta, and the *torricelli* of Cieza—were simply *Inti-huatana.* This conclusion is supported by the negative fact that no remains of such structures as he describes now exist on the hill of Carmenca or any of the others around Cuzco.

Turning again to Garcilasso (Book II) we find this:—

They had likewise observed the equinoctials; for in the month of March, when they reaped their maize or Indian wheat, they celebrated their harvest with joy and feasting, which at Cuzco they kept in the *Colcan,* otherwise called the Garden of the Sun.   At the equinoctial of September, they observed one of their four principal feasts, which were dedicated to the Sun, which they called *Citua Raymir;* and then to denote the precise day of the equinoctial, they had erected pillars of the finest marble, in the open area, or place before the Temple of the Sun; which when the sun came near the line, the priests daily watched and attended to observe what shadow the pillars cast: and to make it the more exact they fixed on them a gnomon, like the pin of a dial, so that so soon as the Sun at its rising came to dart a direct shadow by it, and that at its height or midday the pillar made no shade, but was enlightened on all sides; they then concluded that the sun was entered the equinoctial line.

The Quipu or Peruvian Knot Record. Professor L. Leland Locke says:—

The use of knots in cords for the purpose of reckoning and recording numbers seems to have been as universal as the figures of the cat's cradle in the practices of primitive peoples.   Both may be said to be indigenous to all lands in which the arts of spinning, weaving, and dyeing have been cultivated.   In China, knot records are said to have preceded the knowledge of writing.

In more recent times the most remarkable development of knot records took place among the Incas of Peru.   Here is found the anomaly of a people with a highly complex civilization, particularly in governmental machinery, with a wealth of tradition, with a peculiarly rich and expressive language, but with no system of writing, either hieroglyphic or phonetic.

During his researches Professor Locke located forty-nine ancient quipus, of which the American

Museum possesses forty-two. The simplest form of the quipu may be briefly described as a main cord to which a number of pendent cords are attached. These cords, hanging from the main cord, are usually of several different colors. The knots are tied in these pendent cords. The system of tying these knots varied, and if the quipu changed hands it had to be explained. The contrivance is simplicity itself as a supposed case will show. Let us imagine that the owner of a large number of llamas goes from home, for a lengthy stay, leaving a shepherd in charge. In keeping account of the changes in the flock the shepherd may have the blue cord represent the old male llamas, and the red, the old females. The increase and loss in the flock may be shown by other colors, and so on.

All the knots denoting the same number are tied in a horizontal line (parallel to the main cord) across the depending strings. We will say that the line denoting hundreds is two inches below the main cord; the one for tens, two inches below that; and the line for ones, two inches lower. Now, if it is desired to register the loss of eleven old male llamas on our supposed equipu, it would be done by tying a simple knot on the ten line, and another on the one line of the blue cord. Diagrams and labels with the quipus on exhibition in the museum explain the more complicated forms.

Some of the old Spanish historians tell us that history, traditions, poems, etc., were recorded by the keepers of these knotted strings. These statements, which have been widely quoted, are responsible for the common exaggerated notions of the possibilities of the quipu. The truth of the matter is that the

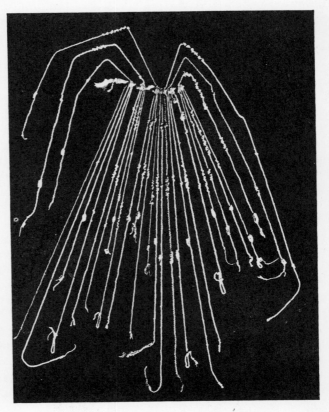

FIG. 49. A Quipu from Chancay, Peru. See diagram on opposite page.

The pendent strands are grouped in fours, each group being tied with a top strand. The top strand sums the numbers on the four pendent strands. In the diagram, Fig. 50, each dot indicates one unit; each ×, a ten, each 0 a hundred, and ⊚ indicates a thousand.

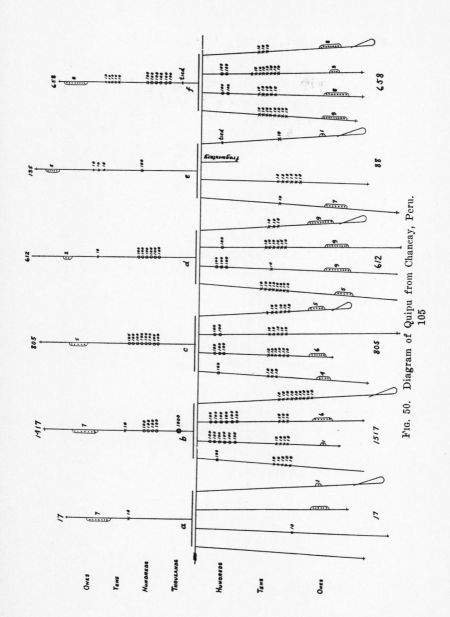

Fig. 50. Diagram of Quipu from Chancay, Peru.

105

quipu was simply used to record the numbers of persons, animals, the quantity of grain, cloth, etc.

The quipu, as a means of keeping accounts, has not entirely disappeared in Peru, as Uhle, Bandelier, and the Countess von Bayern report finding it still in use by the shepherds. These modern quipus are very simple affairs consisting of a short cord with only a very few pendent strands (Figs. 49, 50). It will be seen that in this particular quipu the pendent cords are grouped in fours, each group having a top cord that sums the numbers on the four pendent strands.

In the first group the second cord has one knot on the ten line, the third has six on the one line, and the fourth one on the one line; making seventeen in all. The top cord shows seventeen also, *viz.*, one on the ten line, and seven above the one line. It is a sort of double entry bookkeeping. In the second group, as will be seen, there is a discrepancy of one hundred, which may be due to a mistake of the keeper or to the age and condition of the specimen. One of the cords in the fifth group is missing. The others give the same sums on their top and bottom cords. This specimen may be taken as the highest development of the quipu, as only a few of them have the top cords. There is a great variety in the grouping of the pendent cords, six occurring frequently, while many have these strands attached to the main cord singly.

Medicines and Surgery. Garcilasso, the old Inca historian, quaintly says:—

They had gained so much knowledge in physic as to know that bleeding and purging were necessary evacuation; the blood they drew from the legs and arms or forehead; and because they were not acquainted with the anatomy of the veins they opened that which was nearest to the pain. . . . Their lancet was made of a sharp-pointed flint set at the end of a small cane, which being laid on the vein, with a gentle fillip cuts it with less pain than our ordinary lancets do. (Book 2, Chapter XII.)

He further states that they used for a purge a small white root resembling a turnip, which they beat to a powder, and took with water. The sap of the molle tree was used to heal fresh wounds; the herb called *Chillca* when heated, for pains in the joints; tobacco in the form of snuff for colds; the herb called *matecclu* for the eyes. He says:—

The Indians who were my relatives used divers other herbs, but the names and qualities of them I cannot remember. The bark and flowers of the Chinchona plant were used as a febrifuge. The large number of trephined skulls found in the graves and the pottery figures showing men whose feet have been amputated attest to the advance they had made in surgery.

Trephining was done with a piece of obsidian or sharp stone. After the advent of the Spaniards the Indian medicinemen used a piece of broken bottle, a knife, chisel, or any sharp implement. Fig. 52 shows the famous Squier skull from an Inca cemetery in the Valley of Yucay, in the E. G. Squier collection, now belonging to the American Museum. Previous to this find, it was not known to the scientific world that trephining was practised in Peru in ancient times. M. Broca, after a critical examination of this

FIG. 51. Peruvian Lancet.

skull, presented a paper to the Anthropological Society of Paris. This paper is too long to quote in full, but the following are the first three paragraphs:—

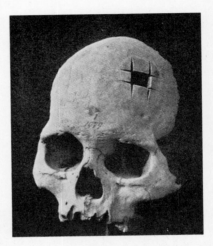

FIG. 52. A Case of Trephining, the famous Squier Skull. The operation was doubtless performed with a piece of obsidian or a sharp stone.

The walls of the skull are very thick, and it presents characteristics which could only belong to an Indian of Peru. And I shall proceed to show that the trepanning was practised during life.

Upon the left side of the external plate of the frontal bone there is a large white spot, quite regular, almost round, or rather slightly elliptical, forty-two millimeters long and forty-seven broad. The outlines of this spot are not irregular or sinuous. The surface is smooth, and presents the appearance of an entirely normal bone. Around this, to the edges, the general color of the skull is notably browner, and is perforated by a great number of small holes, caused by the dilation of the canaliculi. The line of demarkation between the smooth and cribriform surfaces is abrupt, and it is perfectly certain that the smooth surface had been denuded of its periosteum several days before death. It is thus, in truth, that denudations of the cranium behave. In the denuded points, the superficial layer of the external table, deprived of vessels, and thus deprived of life, undergoes no change, and preserves its normal structure; while the surrounding parts, in undergoing the effects of traumatic inflammation, become the seat of the ostitis.

After considering the development of these perforations (porosites) of the external table of the denuded surface, it seems to me impossible to admit that the subject could have survived the denudation less than seven or eight days. M. Nélaton, who examined the specimen, thinks he may have survived fifteen days. (Squier, Appendix A.)

FIG. 53. Prehistoric Surgery: Pottery vessels showing amputation of the foot (at the left) and the placing of a cap over the stump. In Fig. 48 one of the dancing figures wears such a stump.

In Peru, where clubs with star-shaped heads of stone and copper, and slings for throwing stones were in common use, fracture of the skull must have been of frequent occurrence, and trephining was often resorted to in such cases. It is altogether probable that the operation was also performed on account of some religious belief.

Amputation of the foot seems to have been a common surgical operation in the coast region, as a

number of pottery human figures in the Museum's
collection represent men who have lost one or both
feet.   These figures show the skin drawn over the
stump, as it would be by a surgeon today (Fig. 53).
It seems highly probable that this operation was
made necessary by a small sand flea (*Eremita*

Fig. 54.   Pottery Figure of a Man examining the Sole of his Foot
from which the Eggs of a Small Sand Flea have been extracted.

analoga), which is very common in the desert parts
of the Peruvian coast, and which burrows into the
sole of the foot to deposit its egg sack.   This must
be extracted whole, for if it is ruptured serious
trouble will follow, even to the loss of the foot.   The
pottery figure in Fig. 54 shows a man looking at the
sole of his foot, in which we see the depressions from
which egg sacks have been removed.

Fig. 53 also shows a man fitting a cup-shaped extension to the stump to replace his lost foot. If we look at Fig. 48 we find one of the dancers wearing this same device.

Narcotics. The dried leaves of the coca plant (*Erythroxylum coca,* Lamarck), with the addition of a little lime, were chewed exactly as is the betel nut in the East. Indian carriers always have a coca bag slung at their side, and if given a good supply of these leaves will carry a heavy burden over the mountains for days with little or no food. Around the necks of mummies we generally find well-filled coca bags placed there by thoughtful relatives, that the journey to the next world may be pleasant. The very useful local anesthetic, cocaine, is derived from coca leaves. Tobacco was well known to the Peruvians, yet, it seems to have only been used as a medicine, in the form of snuff.

Chicha, a kind of beer, made from maize, was the national drink when the Spaniards entered the country, and has lost none of its popularity since that time. In all the festive gatherings of the Indians the drinking of *chicha* is still the chief feature of the occasion, and the ceremonies, whether religious or otherwise, seldom end until all are completely intoxicated.

Sayings of the Wise. Inca traditions attribute many wise sayings to the Inca Viracocha who is generally believed to have reigned about one hundred years before the time of Huayna Capac. The following is related by Garcilasso (Book V, Chap. XXIX) on the authority of Blas Valera:—

Parents are oftentimes the cause of ruin to their children, when either they educate them with such fondness, that they never cross

them in their wills, or desires, but suffer them to act and do whatso-
ever they please, whereby they become so corrupt in the manners of
their infancy that vice grows ripe with them at the years of man-
hood.   Others, on the contrary, are so severe and cruel to their children that they break the tenderness of their spirits and affright them
from learning, discouraging them in that manner by menaces and
lectures of a supercilious pedant, that their wits are abased, and
despair of attaining to knowledge and virtue. The way is to keep
an indifferent mean between both, by which youth becomes valiant
and hardy in war, and wise and political in time of peace.

If this saying is rightly attributed to Viracocha it
shows that the great problem now agitating parents,
as to the best way of bringing up their children, also
troubled the Incas many years ago.

Language.   Many languages and dialects were
spoken in Peru, but on account of our very imperfect
knowledge of the subject, it will be possible to dis-
cuss them only in a very general way.   At the time
of the Conquest the languages used over the largest
areas were the Quechua and the Aymara.

Quechua, the language of the Incas, was spoken in
most localities, from Quito almost to the southern
confines of the empire, in the region about Cuzco,
and to the east of Lake Titicaca.   It had also been
introduced among some tribes to the south into what
is now the Argentine Republic.

Aymara was the language of the Collao, the region
northwest, west, and south of Lake Titicaca.

A large and powerful nation on the northern coast,
having its capital and center at Chan Chan, near
Trujillo, spoke a language which is generally called
Chimu.   Thirty years ago it was said that many of
the inhabitants of the little village of Santa Rosa,
near Eten, still spoke the original Chimu language.

Notwithstanding the remarkable cultural advance made by the Peruvians they had no hieroglyphic or other form of written language.

Garcilasso (Royal Commentaries, Book VII, Chap. 1) says that a policy of the Incas which conduced to the regular government of their empire was a command laid upon all their vassals to learn the language of the court (Quechua). Certain masters were appointed to instruct the people. The reasons for commanding the use of a common language were, first, to avoid the multitude of interpreters which would be necessary for understanding the various languages spoken within the jurisdiction of that great empire; second, the Inca took particular satisfaction in addressing his subjects directly instead of through an interpreter. This is interesting in many ways; for one thing, it suggests how uniformity in language may be brought about.

CHAPTER VII

SEQUENCE OF CULTURES

SINCE the preceding pages were written in 1924
some significant investigations have been under-
taken, the results of which suggest certain time-
relations between the important cultures characterized in the Introduction. These pre-Inca cultures
may be comprehended under locality names such as
Nazca, Chimu, Chavin, Trujillo, Tiahuanaco, and
Ica. The outstanding problem is to determine the
time-relations between these several cultures, and
while no final statement can be made at this time, the
main outline of Andean prehistory is suggested in
the researches of Uhle, Bandelier, Kroeber, Tello,
Jijon y Caamaño, Means, and others, all of which
are summarized in a recent article in *Natural His-*
tory by Professor R. L. Olson, from which the following has been extracted:—

When Pizarro and his band of 190 warriors landed
at Tumbez in 1532, the greater part of the modern
republics of Ecuador, Peru, Bolivia, and Chile was
a powerful empire—the dominion of the Quechua
people. Over it ruled Inca, supreme emperor, demi-
god, offspring of the sun. About the year 1000 the
Quechuas were a small tribe living in the region of
Cuzco, just starting on the career of conquest which
in five centuries culminated in an empire stretching
the 2,300 miles from northern Ecuador to middle
Chile. Not alone in size was this empire impressive.
The splendor of its templed pyramids, the grandly
conceived works of irrigation, the well-knit fabric of
its society and government—all these filled the more
thoughtful among the conquering Spaniards with an

admiration which almost amounted to awe. As a consequence the word "Inca" is surrounded by a glamor that has resulted in giving the Quechuas (Incas) credit for more than their share of the achievements which mark Andean civilization.

A thousand years before the Incas began their conquests, Peru's Coast and Highland had already seen the beginnings of civilizations take root in their soil. The next few centuries saw these cultures flourish for a time, their arts reach a high plane of excellence, then fade. On the cold bleak shores of Lake Titicaca arose the mighty structures of Tiahuanaco—center and probable fount of the Megalithic Empire whose territory was perhaps as far-flung as that of the Inca Empire. But Tiahuanaco was already in ruins when the early Incas first came that way. Its heroic sculpture and art had a subsequent flowering far to the north at Chavin and at other centers. Centuries before the period of this Megalithic Empire, the coastal plain in Peru was the seat of other civilizations. In the region of Nazca lived a people already versed in the arts of agriculture, ceramics, and weaving, and on the northern coast lived the Chimu, a people equally conversant with these pursuits. The pottery and textiles of these early periods excel those of subsequent epochs in beauty, technique, and decorative excellence.

Aside from a few vague hints of rude fisher-folk living along the ocean and of primitive hunters in the Sierra, we are in almost complete ignorance of the long history which must lie back of these complex civilizations of the Nazca and Chimu peoples. It is against all precedent and logic that highly developed civilizations such as these should be without cultural predecessors.

Only in recent years have systematic scientific studies been made by archaeologists, notably by Uhle and Bandelier, more recently by Kroeber, Tello, Jijon y Caamaño, and others. Their findings have been used in the study of older collections by Means, Lehmann, Joyce, d'Harcourt, and Schmidt, to mention only a few. Each of these has, in one way or another, tried to sketch in broad outlines the historical pictures of the past. It seems worth while to present a composite of these reconstructions—to pick out the more salient and the more certain figures in each and unite them in a running sketch of the various epochs and peoples which have passed across the stage, the background of which is the Andean highland and the Pacific coast of South America.

What kind of people first moved into the Andean country we do not know. Probably they were primitive hunters and perhaps during this same period the Coast was inhabited by rude folk who lived mainly on fish and shell fish. At any rate, we may assume that several thousands of years ago the first settlers were drifting southward from Central America along the Coast and Highland in a series of waves. But the remains of these pioneers are either difficult to find or we have not yet learned how to locate them.

A long period of time now passes before we get the next glimpse of human history in this area. But the next picture is clear and surprising. Along the southern coast of Peru, in the region of Nazca, and a little later in the Trujillo region of the northern coast, appear civilizations of a high order. Here, as elsewhere in the area, our reconstructions of culture are based in the main on ceramic and textile remains, the figures and scenes depicted, less on the residuum of stray objects, of refuse deposits, and so on. The definite characteristics of the artistic elements enable us to identify the materials of these civilizations from others with considerable certainty. Though the early Nazca culture is probably earlier than that of the Trujillo section (seat of the Early Chimu civilization), our knowledge of the latter is more complete.

We can picture the early Chimu as a people living largely by means of agriculture, with maize, beans, potatoes, and cotton as the principal domesticated plants. To bring water to irrigate the dry alluvial fans, many miles of great canals and ditches were constructed. The social structure was a complex one, with chiefs, priests, warriors, commoners, and slaves forming the strata of society. A pantheon of deities was worshiped, with the puma-god the most important. Great truncated pyramids were erected to serve as the bases for temples and the residence of high dignitaries of state. The art of weaving was highly developed, decorative fabrics and poncho-like shirts being fairly numerous in the remains which have been preserved. Pottery is characterized by pleasing forms decorated chiefly in reds on a cream slip, and by "portrait jars." The painted decorations, done in graceful lines, often depict scenes from the life of the period. It is from these formally realistic decorations that we are able to reconstruct the culture of the people.

In the valley of Nazca during a slightly earlier period there flourished a culture basically like that of the Chimu. Scarcely an item in the decorative art of Nazca seems related to that of the Chimu, but we can reasonably infer a genetic connection between the civilizations, for in features other than art there are many similarities. Nazca pottery is characterized by elaborate polychrome decorations, the chief motifs being flowers, birds, fishes, trophy heads, and a monster-deity with the characteristics of a composite feline-serpent. Textiles are often embroidered with elaborate representations of this same being. Nazca art is so much given to conventionalization and to the depiction of mythological fantasy that we are unable to reconstruct the everyday life of the people with the same sureness as in the case of the early Chimu.

The culture of Nazca is the earliest of which we have knowledge, but that of the Trujillo area is only a little later in point of time. Both seem to be restricted to the forbidding deserts of the coastal plain —a region so unpromising that only somewhat civilized peoples could cope with natural conditions. The next epoch opens in the Highland, in the great plateaus which lie between the ranges of the Andes at elevations of 8,000 to 14,000 feet.

We do not know what events took place in the Highland during the time of these early Chimu and Nazca periods. But somewhere near their end a unique civilization was arising at Tiahuanaco on the cold barren shores of Lake Titicaca. Somewhat crude at first, this culture soon flourished in the classic style of Tiahuanaco. The rainy climate of the Sierra soon destroys such remains as textiles and other objects which decay under moist conditions, and we must content ourselves with the study of architectural styles, stone sculptures, and ceramics. These show the Tiahuanaco culture to be quite distinct from that of Early Nazca and Early Chimu. The feline deity of the Coast was reverenced as well as the condor-god and the sun. The "weeping god" of the gateway and other stone sculpture of the ruins of Tiahuanaco are type examples of the lithic art of the era. The architecture is massive in design, truly Megalithic in scope. The Tiahuanaco ruins show a city with its temples and other structures laid out according to a grand plan, impressive in a way quite different from the great adobe brick pyramids of the coast. The latter exhibit only a prodigious amount of labor expended to little ultimate avail: the Megalithic builders would have reared a splendid city with less effort.

Pottery forms are sometimes reminiscent of those of Nazca, but the decorative elements are often human and animal faces and figures which are very unlike the Nazca type. The feline and condor gods are often shown having human bodies. The colors employed are reds, blacks, and less often, whites. Even where these are the same basic hues used in Chimu and Nazca ware, their values and intensities are of a different order. While Tiahuanaco art is restrained and severe, that of Nazca is elaborate, almost flamboyant. A fairly constant detail of Tiahuanaco art are the "tear drops" or "tear streaks" that decorate the cheeks of faces.

Stone sculpture or pottery remains, reminiscent of the Tiahuanaco style, are found from the Diaguita area in the Argentine to San Augustin in southern Colombia. At Chavin in central Peru a secondary center sprang up, probably toward the end of the classical Tiahuanaco period. Here severity of line and simplicity of execution gave way to complex figures with single elements of the parent motifs often used to decorate a field. Conventionalized puma and condor heads executed in the Chavin manner are found in pottery of the early Chimu period, giving proof of reciprocal influences and of commerce between Coast and Sierra. We have certain proof that Early Nazca precedes Tiahuanaco. Chavin art, difficult to analyze as a predecessor of Tiahuanaco, is more explicable as a derivative. Since the Chavin style is associated in graves and ruins with that of Chimu, we are justified in placing Early Chimu as later than Early Nazca.

Toward or at the end of the Nazca period, pottery and textiles in the style of Tiahuanaco are to be found in coastal sites from northern Chile to northern Peru. Certain of these exhibit the style in all its vigor, but other finds show a degeneration in both technique and execution. To this period on the coast the name "Epigonal" or "Tiahuanacoid" (derived from Tiahuanaco) has been given. Perhaps this degeneration is to be explained by lack of further stimulation from the parent culture. A puzzling feature of the Tiahuanaco-Chimu-Chavin relationship is that both Tiahuanaco and Chavin ware are found with Early Chimu. This might seem to indicate that Chavin and Tiahuanaco forms probably came as an influence from along the coast to the south, while those of Chavin had only to traverse the short distance across the western range of the Andes. The Tiahuanaco influence started to spread earlier but the time-distance element resulted in its reaching the Chimu area at roughly the same time as the Chavin influence.

The Tiahuanaco culture (or its hypothetical predecessors) had enriched its world by the cultural gifts of bronze, the potato, the domesticated llama, a distinctive architecture and art, and then passed into oblivion until resurrected by the archaeological studies of a stranger race.

At the present time we are able to reconstruct but little of the series of events which had been taking place in the northern Highland of Peru during the Tiahuanaco period. In that area there has been little archaeological work done, and the probable relationship of the Megalithic cultures of Tiahuanaco and Chavin to those of Colombia and beyond is indicated largely by inference. We are without data which might give clues to the possible spread of the Megalithic cultures over this northern region of the Peruvian Highland.

In the northern Sierra almost all of the ruins are found at high altitudes, in a belt of dense vegetation which makes exploration and excavation difficult. Pottery remains are hard to find, undisturbed graves are harder. A preliminary reconnaissance in this region in 1930 by the writer yielded the following results:—

Fortresses, temples, houses, and other structures are in a type of stone architecture basically like that of Tiahuanaco and Chavin. Certain villages are composed entirely of circular stone structures some ten to thirty feet in diameter with stone roofs of a corbelled dome type. Other villages show both round and square houses with similarly domed

roofs. Since a domed stone roof is more in keeping
with a circular than a square house, we may assume
the former to be the earlier type. The dead were
buried in niches in the walls, in caves, or in house-
like tombs built against the faces of cliffs. Burials
were flexed, the bodies wrapped in cloth. Contacts
with the tropical forest or with the coastal belt are
indicated by the presence of cotton fabrics and of
coca. The pottery is a heavy somewhat crude ware,
usually undecorated. Decoration is by appliquéd
strips of clay, by crudely modeled animal figures, or
by curious spiral designs in a dark red on a creamy-
red background. These bits of data permit no more
than the bare statement that this northern highland
culture represents that of Chavin-Tiahuanaco in an
attenuated form. The round house forms are reminiscent of the "chullpas" of the Titicaca region
which seem to relate to a period following Tiahuanaco.

Following the decline of the Tiahuanaco period in
the southern Highland and later on the Coast, the
picture is once more obscured. The coastal cultures
seem to have gone through a period of stagnation.
The refinements of the Chimu and Nazca arts and
the strength of the Tiahuanaco-Epigonal style are
lacking in the new forms which appear. On the
northern and central coast from Chicama to Lurin
there appears a red-white-black pottery which seems
related to that of Recuay in the Callejon de Huay-
las. This is perhaps best interpreted as a later
counterpart of the early Chavin-Chimu influence.
The classical (Early) Chimu style shows little af-
finity to these later coastal styles. It seems that the
Recuoid ware, a peculiar cursive style, and the later

polished black ware may be influences radiating from the Chiclayo-Leche region. Unfortunately there has not been sufficient work in this section to establish relationships with the Chimu-Chavin style.

About this time the Chimu culture had a revival. Perhaps a new political organization under the kings known as "Great Chimu" was related to the conquests which carried the Late Chimu culture over the entire coast from Huacho to Piura. This is the period of the building of Chan Chan, "capital" of the Chimu kingdom and largest city in prehistoric Peru. This late Chimu period persisted until the irresistible conquests of the Incas carried them to the northern coast about a century before the coming of the Spaniards.

On the southern coast the fading of the Tiahuanaco influence was followed after a time by the growth of a new culture which was centered in the valley of Ica, just north of Nazca. Here careful work and analysis by Uhle, Kroeber, and Strong have enabled us to establish the sequence: Nazca-Epigonal-Middle Ica-Late Ica-Inca, with considerable certainty. In some respects the characteristics of each style show blended or attenuated forms in the succeeding style or styles. Accordingly we may suppose a continuous history, with the arts of previous periods serving to shape the new cultures. The Ica styles include a number of new vessel forms. Like their predecessors, the Ica vessels are decorated in three or four colors, with red, black, white, and slate predominating but often blended with still others. Ica decorations, like those of the Epigonal, lack the firmness and precision which characterize the Nazca style. The designs are mainly geometric, probably textile patterns applied to pottery. Traces of the Ica influence may be found as far north as Chincha. Like Late Chimu, the Late Ica civilization persists down to the Inca period.

About the same time as Middle Ica new developments were taking place in the region of Chincha-Cañete to the north of Pisco. The pottery forms vary, exhibiting Late Chimu and Ica traits with other forms in a local "Chincha" style. Back of this period undoubtedly lie others as yet undiscovered or at best unplaced as to time. The Chincha period at its end merges with the Inca.

It is now necessary to return again to events in the Highland. Tiahuanaco had been lying in ruins for probably several centuries. The Megalithic Empire had, however, enjoyed a brief renaissance at Chavin and other centers. Now these centers of influence as well had gone the way of their cultural mother. A period about which we know almost nothing had endured for a long span of time in the Highland.

But there was living in the upper valley of the Urubamba a small tribe, the Quechua, which was destined to play a brilliant, though ultimately unfortunate, part in the history of the native races. Perhaps the Quechuas (Incas) had been a subject people under the Megalithic Empire. Tradition concerning them begins about the year 1000, when the more or less mythical Manco Ccapac was "Inca." (The word "Inca" was the title of the ruler, but through an erroneous popular usage has come to apply to the entire Quechua people and to the empire which they conquered.) This was only some five hundred years before the Spanish conquest—sufficiently close to the horizon of history to permit us to place some faith in Inca history as set forth in their oral traditions.

Manco Ccapac and his successor made their people supreme in the vicinity of Cuzco. The third Inca, Lloque Yupanqui, extended his territory to the south as far as Lake Titicaca. There followed a series of notable rulers each of whom extended the boundaries of empire during his reign. At the end of the reign of Pachacutec, who died about 1478, the empire had been extended well into what is now the Argentine, into northern Peru to Cajamarca, and on the coast over the territory of the Chimu. Under the next Incas, Tupoc Inca Yupanqui and his successor, Huayna Ccapac, successful campaigns brought the boundaries of the empire nearly to Colombia in the north and to the Rio Maule, perhaps to the Rio Bio Bio, on the central coast of Chile—a distance of some 2300 miles, an empire larger than that of Rome at the time of Caesar's birth. Huayna Ccapac died at Quito in 1525. His heir, Ninan Cuyuchi, died soon after, and Huascar, second in line, now became Inca. But his right to the throne was disputed by the ill-fated Atahualpa, an illegitimate son. The civil war which followed weakened the empire and divided the loyalty of the people. Atahualpa was finally successful, but at the moment of victory news came to him at Cajamarca that a body of strange and mighty men had landed on the coast. This was November, 1532. Pizarro marched to Cajamarca, took Atahualpa prisoner by a ruse, and within a year had captured Cuzco and was in complete control of the Inca realm. Except for a series of increasingly futile rebellions, resis-

tance was over, the Inca part in the drama was
ended. The New World had lost its last chance to
remain for a time free from the devastating effects
of European civilization.

The Inca genius was one for conquest and political organization rather than of excellence in arts
and crafts. Their pottery has a certain grace of
form but is not so pleasing as the best of Chimu or
Tiahuanaco ware. Textiles are colorful in a gaudy
sort of way. Inca architecture may be said to follow the Megalithic tradition without showing the
restrained grandeur of Tiahuanaco. In the coastal
belt the structures of the period are far inferior to
the impressive masses of the Chimu pyramids.

In some respects the Inca scheme of political
organization was like that of the Romans. A vast
system of roads was built in both the rugged highland and desert coast land. At regular intervals
along these highways "tambos" or storehouses
were built where supplies for travelers and for the
army were kept. Messengers were constantly on
duty at these points ready to relay messages from
one part of the country to another. When a new
area was conquered, a part of the inhabitants were
transplanted to older parts of the empire and loyal
subjects were moved in to take their place. This
was to guard against rebellion and to disseminate
the Quechua tongue over the conquered territory.
The religious and social institutions of subject tribes
were allowed to persist. A temple to the sun was
usually erected near the foreign places of worship
but there was never an attempt to stamp out the
prevalent beliefs. This is in keeping with the toler-

ant attitude of most peoples other than those of the white race toward other beliefs.

A hierarchy of religious and civil officials served as mentors of social, political, and religious activities. At the head of these stood the Inca, the ruler-god, descendant of the sun god, and supreme authority in all matters. The empire and its people were his by divine right. Aside from houses and personal effects, there was little private ownership. Since long before the days of the Incas, the people of the empire had been organized in *allyus* or clans which owned the lands. The leaders of these *allyus* assigned certain fields to individuals to till for one year only. The following year there was a reassignment. The Incas wove this ancient social organization into their political system. A portion of the produce of each community was taken over by the state to satisfy the needs of religion and government.

The Incaic system was a form of communism curiously blended with a thorough but benign despotism. One governmental department looked after the conservation of wild animals, another safeguarded the forests from needless exploitation. A corps of engineers planned and built cities, temples, and bridges. Census takers annually noted the amount of a man's crops, the number of his children, his ability for work. Certain likely children were trained to be soldiers, others to be priests, still others to fill posts in the administrative service of the government. The system seems to be one instance where the theory of state communism was applied with a measure of success. It was, of course, built upon concepts of

property and personal rights quite different from
our own.

Many, perhaps most of "the great things which
were found in this kingdom" (to use Cieza's
words), were not the works of the Incas, but, as we
have seen, are to be ascribed to civilizations which
existed long before. Indeed, the entire course of
Peruvian history almost seems to have run contrary
to progressive evolution. The earliest civilization,
that of Nazca, excels all subsequent cultures in the
numbers of colors used in ceramics and textiles, in
control of technical processes in those arts, and in
complexity of design. The somewhat later Early
Chimu pottery excels in grace of decorative lines
and delicacy of color. The art of the next major
period, that of Tiahuanaco, has the merit of strength
in architecture and in pottery design, but more often
the strength of design in ceramic becomes crudity of
downright sloppiness. In both highland and coast
its later examples run to flamboyancy or to original
motifs broken up so that conventionalized parts of
earlier figures serve to decorate an entire field. The
objects surviving from the Inca period can lay small
claim to artistic excellence.

In its broader outlines there is hardly any
doubt of the correctness of the sequence: Nazca-
Early Chimu → Tiahuanaco-Epigonal-Chavin → Late
Chimu-Ica → Inca. The sequences and relationships
within these periods may be, and are, still open to
some question. But regardless of how we place
these minor epochs the larger development still remains one of retrogression from the superior to the
inferior. On the material side of life this is true
only in part. The early (but not the earliest) pyra-

mids of the Chimu period excel those of the later, and the Tiahuanaco style has claims to superiority. But on the other hand, grander irrigation works, cities of larger size, and a more varied food supply characterize the later periods. We cannot, of course, subject the social, political, and religious institutions of the several periods to a similar analysis because of the difficulty of reconstructing intangibles from archaeological data.

At the time of the Spanish conquest, Peru seemed ready to enter upon a new era of development. We have already mentioned how the Inca Empire had welded together a large number of smaller states, related yet distinct in their civilizations. Perhaps the best of the arts of these would have been conserved and unified. Trade by sea with Central America and Mexico seems already to have been established. Peruvian civilizations excelled in the manual arts, those of the Maya area in the intellectual, and a closer contact would have stimulated developments in both areas. The northerners have already benefited by borrowing knowledge of the bronze technique, perhaps the Incas would have learned the art of writing and erecting dated monuments. A slight expansion to the north would have brought the Inca and Chibcha civilizations into contact and this might have resulted in still greater acceleration.

The civilizations of Middle America—Aztec, Maya, Chibcha, and Inca—had advanced far without possessing certain rather fundamental arts and inventions. Nowhere in Middle America was iron known. Bronze furnished a substitute but is inferior for most purposes. Transport was handicapped by lack of knowledge of the wheel. The task of moving the great stones of the Megalithic structures, some weighing twenty or thirty tons, was accomplished without it. The New World is lacking in any animals as tractable and sturdy as the horse and ox of the Old World. The llama was used as a pack animal but it can carry only small burdens, is not adapted for riding and is not suited to low altitudes. The Aztec and Maya possessed the rudiments of writing, an elaborate system of enumeration, and a splendid calendric scheme, but knowledge of them had only begun to filter into South America. Splendid as were the achievements of the civilizations of prehistoric Peru in the way of agriculture, the arts, and political and social schemes, they were hindered by ignorance of these basic traits. Except for these they were perhaps as civilized as their European conquerors. But take these traits—writing, iron, the wheel—out of our own cultural scheme and we find ourselves unable to carry on our modern life. The wonder is that the ancient Peruvians, lacking these, had progressed so far.

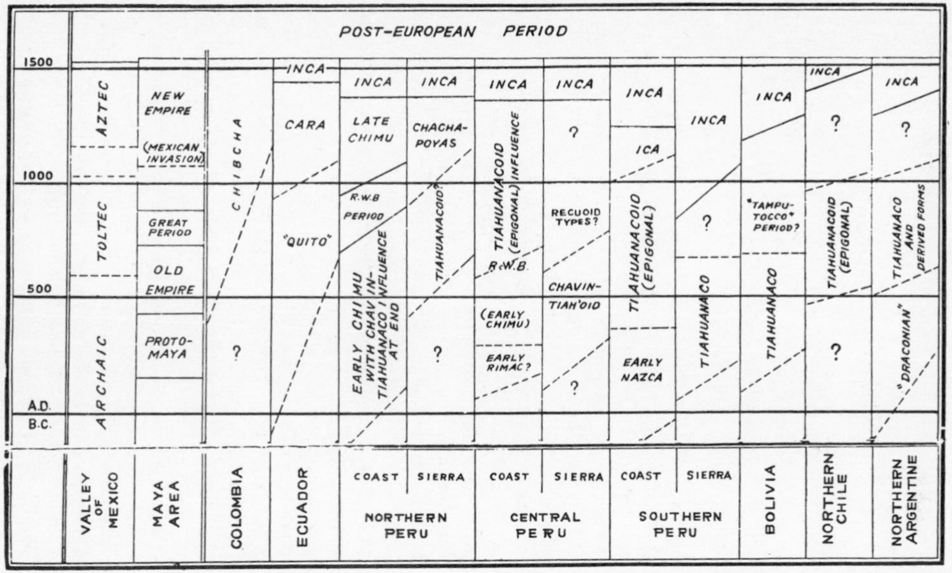

FIG. 55. The Sequence of Cultures in the Andean Highland and Pacific Coast of South America. The diagram summarizes the known and inferred developments during the fifteen centuries of which we have knowledge.—After R. L. Olson.

131

BIBLIOGRAPHY

The following works are but a small part of the extensive bibliography of Peru, but will be found sufficient for any one wishing to acquire a general acquaintance with the subject.

ACOSTA, JOSÉ DE. The Naturall and Morall Historie of the East and West Indies. Edited by Clements R. Markham. London, 1880.

BAESSLER, ARTHUR. Altperuanische Metallgeräte. Berlin, 1906.

Ancient Peruvian Art. 4 vols. Berlin and New York, 1902–1903.

BANDELIER, ADOLPH FRANCIS. The Islands of Titicaca and Koati. New York, 1910.

VON BAYERN, PRINZESSIN THERESE. Reisestudien aus dem Westlichen Südamerika. 2 vols. Berlin, 1908.

BINGHAM, HIRAM. Inca Land. Boston, 1922.

Machu Picchu, A Citadel of the Incas. New Haven, 1930.

The Story of Machu Picchu. (National Geographic Magazine, February, 1915.)

BOMAN, ERIC. Antiquités de la Région Andine, de la République Argentine, et du Désert d'Atacama. 2 vols. Paris, 1908.

CIEZA DE LEON, PEDRO DE. The Travels of Pedro de Cieza de Leon A.D. 1532–1550, contained in the First Part of his Chronicle of Peru. Translated and edited by Clements R. Markham. London, 1864.

The Second Part of the Chronicle of Peru. Translated and edited by Clements R. Markham. London, 1883.

CONWAY, SIR MARTIN. The Bolivian Andes; a Record of Climbing and Exploration in the Cordillera Real in the Years 1898 and 1900. New York and London, 1901.

CRAWFORD, M. D. C. Peruvian Textiles. (Anthropological Papers, American Museum of Natural History, vol. 12, part 3, 1915.)

Peruvian Fabrics. (Anthropological Papers, American Museum of Natural History, vol. 12, part 4, 1915.)

DORSEY, GEORGE A. Archaeological Investigations on the Island of
La Plata, Ecuador (Publication No. 56, Field Columbian
Museum, Chicago, 1901).

ENOCK, C. REGINALD. Peru. London, 1912.

GARCILASSO DE LA VEGA. The Royal Commentaries of Peru. Edited
by Sir Paul Rycaut. London, 1688.

HARCOURT, RAOUL AND MARIE D'. La Céramique Ancienne du Pérou.
Paris, 1924.

Les Tissus Indiens du Vieux Pérou. Paris, 1924.

La Musique des Incas et ses Survivances. 2 vols. Paris, 1925.

HOLMES, W. H. Textile Fabrics of Ancient Peru (Bulletin 7,
Bureau of Ethnology, Washington, 1899).

HUTCHINSON, THOMAS J. Two Years in Peru, with Explorations of
Its Antiquities. 2 vols. London, 1873.

JOYCE, THOMAS A. South American Archaeology. New York, 1912.

KROEBER, A. L. Archaeological Explorations in Peru, Part II. The
Northern Coast (Field Museum of Natural History, Anthro-
pology, Memoirs, vol. 2, no. 2, Chicago, 1930).

LEHMANN, WALTER. The Art of Old Peru. Assisted by Heinrich
Doering. Publication of the Ethnological Institute of the
Ethnographical Museum, Berlin. Berlin, London, New
York, 1924.

LOCKE, L. L. The Ancient Quipu or Peruvian Knot Record (American Museum of Natural History, 1923).

MARKHAM, CLEMENTS R. The Incas of Peru. New York, 1910.

MEAD, CHARLES W. Technique of Some South American Feather-
work (Anthropological Papers, American Museum of Natural History, vol. 1, part 1, 1907).

Prehistoric Bronze in South America (Anthropological Papers,
American Museum of Natural History, vol. 12, part 2,
1915).

Peruvian Art (Guide Leaflet No. 46, American Museum of Natural History, 1919).

The Musical Instruments of the Incas (Anthropological Papers,
American Museum of Natural History, vol. 15, part 3,
1924).

MEANS, PHILIP AINSWORTH. Peruvian Textiles. Examples of the
Pre-Incaic Period. With an Introduction by Joseph Breck.
(Metropolitan Museum of Art, New York, 1930).

Ancient Civilizations of the Andes. New York and London,
1931.

134   OLD CIVILIZATIONS OF INCA LAND

MIDDENDORF, E. W. Peru. 3 vols. Berlin, 1894–1895.

NORDENSKIÖLD, BARON ERLAND. The Copper and Bronze Ages in South America. Gothenburg, 1921.

The Secret of the Peruvian Quipus. Gothenburg, 1925.

OLSON, RONALD L. Old Empires of the Andes. (Natural History, vol. 31, no. 1, pp. 3–22, 1931.)

PIZARRO, PEDRO. Relation of the Discovery and Conquest of the Kingdom of Peru. Translated and edited by P. A. Means. New York (Cortes Society), 2 vols. 1921.

PRESCOTT, WILLIAM H. History of the Conquest of Peru. 2 vols. New York, 1847.

RAIMONDI, ANTONIO. El Peru. 6 vols. Lima, 1874–1913.

RECK, HUGO. Geographie und Statistik der Republik Bolivia (Petermann's Mittheilungen, 1865).

REISS, W., AND STÜBEL, A. The Necropolis of Ancon in Peru. 3 vols. Berlin, 1880–1887.

SCHMIDT, MAX. Kunst und Kultur von Peru. Berlin, 1929.

SELER, EDUARD. Peruanische Alterthumer. Berlin, 1893.

SQUIER, E. GEORGE. Incidents of Travel and Exploration in the Land of the Incas. New York, 1877.

TELLO, JULIO C. Antiguo Perú. Lima, 1929.

VON TSCHUDI, JOHANN J. Reisen durch Südamerika. 5 vols. Leipzig, 1868.

UHLE, MAX. Pachacamac. Philadelphia, 1903.

UHLE, MAX, AND STÜBEL, ALPHONS. Die Ruinenstätte von Tiahuanaco im hochlande des Alten Peru. Breslau, 1892.

ULLOA, ANTONIO, AND JUAN, GEORGE. A Voyage to South America. 2 vols. London, 1760.

WIENER, CHARLES. Pérou et Bolivie. Paris, 1880.

INDEX